AI READINESS FOR LEADERS

A Human-Centered Framework

Guide to Future-Proof Your Organization

Dr. Farzana Chohan

Founder & Director: Optimize Excellence, AIArchitect8

AI READINESS FOR LEADERS

Copyright © 2025 by Farzana Chohan

ISBN: 978-1-987931-23-5

Published by AiArchitect818 Press

Dedication

This writing is dedicated to each one of us, to all.

*We have been and we are forward-looking,
intelligent humans.*

*We are leaders, we are organizations and we can
and we will collectively, come together to balance
technology with our humanity.*

Preface – Why This Book, Why Now

I remember sitting in a boardroom as executives debated whether to "buy AI" like a new software suite. What struck me wasn't the lack of interest—it was the lack of understanding. As an advisor, I asked a simple question: "Who in this room feels ready to lead the people who will use it?" Silence. That silence advanced this book. AI readiness isn't about coding—it's about consciousness.

Artificial Intelligence is reshaping leadership faster than any previous revolution. Yet too many organizations still mistake technology adoption for true transformation. Rolling out new AI tools alone won't magically change an organization's trajectory. The real challenge – and opportunity – lies in transforming mindsets and culture alongside deploying new algorithms. In short, **true AI readiness begins not with algorithms but with awareness** – a human awareness at all levels of the organization.

This book was born from that recognition. We've all seen companies rush to implement AI solutions only to stall or backfire because employees weren't on board, processes weren't adjusted, or ethical guardrails were missing. As a leadership advisor, I wrote this guide to help leaders avoid those pitfalls by taking a more pragmatic, people-centric approach. AI can undoubtedly drive efficiency and innovation, but harnessing it requires *leadership* – vision, empathy, clarity – to guide the change.

Why now? Because the window for proactive leadership is narrow. Surveys show that barely 1% of companies consider their AI initiatives "mature," while about 75% have yet to see meaningful returns on their AI investments. The gap isn't in technology – it's in preparedness. Organizations that *do* achieve AI-driven gains approach it holistically: they align AI projects to strategy, invest in upskilling people, build a culture of trust, and ensure responsible use. They recognize that **AI readiness is ultimately human readiness** – a new core leadership competency for the coming decade.

In the following pages, I offer a framework to measure and accelerate your organization's AI readiness in practical, human-centered terms. This is not a technical manual about algorithms; it's a leadership playbook grounded in research, psychology, and real-world experience advising companies, universities, and nonprofits worldwide. Each chapter provides tools, case studies, and reflection exercises so you can translate insight into action. My goal is for you to come away empowered to lead your team into the AI era – *confidently, ethically,* and *intentionally.*

AI is here to stay. The leaders who will thrive are those prepared to continually learn, adapt, and inspire others through this disruption. If you're picking up this book, you've already taken the first step: seeking understanding. I wrote **AI Readiness for Leaders** to be your roadmap from understanding to action. Together, let's navigate this transformation with eyes wide open to both the revolutionary potential of AI and the timeless power of human leadership.

Boardroom Awakening

"I once asked a boardroom full of executives, 'Who here feels ready to lead the people who will use AI?' Silence filled the room. That silence birthed this book."
— *Leadership Insight from Dr. Farzana Chohan*

INTRODUCTION – The Leadership Imperative in the AI Era

During my time on a healthcare organization's advisory board, I watched the CIO present an impressive AI pilot that reduced patient wait times. The CEO leaned forward and said, "Wonderful—but how do we make our clinicians trust it?" That moment crystallized for me that the true challenge in AI transformation isn't algorithms—it's alignment.

"Leaders will not be replaced by AI — but **leaders who fail to embrace AI will be replaced by those who do**." This adage rings truer with each passing day. In the AI era, adaptability isn't just an asset for leadership; it's the defining imperative. The most advanced algorithms mean little without leaders who can integrate them into a compelling vision and culture. Conversely, even the best leaders will struggle if they ignore the new tools and insights AI offers. The message is clear: the future belongs to leaders who can do both – **harness AI's power while amplifying uniquely human strengths**.

This introduction lays the groundwork by presenting the **AI Readiness Spectrum™**, a model to assess an organization's preparedness across three critical domains: **Strategic Readiness, Operational Readiness, and Human Readiness**.

Why these three? Because building an AI-ready company is not just an IT project or a data science exercise – it's a comprehensive transformation of strategy, operations, and mindset. Research consistently shows that companies successful with AI approach it multidimensionally, aligning technology with business goals, upgrading processes and data capabilities, and fostering a receptive culture. The AI Readiness Spectrum™ distills this into a practical diagnostic tool with five maturity stages in each domain.

Imagine a spectrum from organizations utterly unaware of AI's relevance to those fully transformed by AI-driven innovation. Most companies today find themselves somewhere in between – perhaps dabbling in pilot projects but lacking a strategy, or equipped with cutting-edge tools but struggling with cultural resistance. The Spectrum's five stages are: **Unaware** → **Experimental** → **Operational** → **Strategic** → **Transformative**. In Chapter 2, we'll dive deep into what defines each stage and provide a self-assessment matrix so you can pinpoint where your team stands. The aim is not to label, but to illuminate the path forward – the specific gaps to close to reach the next level.

Why focus equally on human factors as on tech and strategy? Because in practice, **AI adoption lives or**

dies by human adoption. Consider that many organizations technically have the infrastructure for AI, yet they remain *organizationally unprepared* – their people don't trust the AI, processes aren't redesigned for it, and leadership hasn't set a clear vision. On the other hand, organizations that cultivate a learning culture and ethical guardrails often accelerate their AI progress, precisely because employees and stakeholders support the changes. One recent study put it succinctly: *The future doesn't belong to those with the most advanced models; it belongs to those who align people, processes, and technology to make those models work.* In other words, AI readiness is as much about hearts and minds as it is about data and code.

Leadership in the AI era means guiding your organization along this spectrum – from early awareness to full transformation – while keeping humans at the center. It means asking not just *"What can AI do?"* but *"What should we do with AI, and how do we bring our people along?"* The coming chapters equip you with frameworks to answer these questions. By the end of this book, you'll be able to assess your current AI readiness, identify priority actions, implement ethical AI practices, build an AI-ready culture, measure ROI, and continually adapt your leadership approach as AI evolves.

The imperative is clear and urgent. Those who wait for "someone else" (perhaps the IT department or a few tech enthusiasts) to drive AI understanding will fall behind. Those who lead on AI – who educate themselves and their teams, who experiment and learn, who integrate AI into strategy and values – will position their organizations to thrive. **Leadership has always been about navigating change**. AI is simply the newest, most rapid, and arguably most profound change leaders have had to navigate in decades. The chapters ahead will ensure you are ready – not just to cope with that change, but to leverage it to future-proof your organization and uplift the people within it.

Let's begin this journey by demystifying AI itself, cutting through the hype to understand what AI truly is (and isn't) and how it can augment (not replace) human intelligence. From there, we'll explore each dimension of readiness in turn. Welcome to the AI Readiness journey – one that will challenge you to grow as a leader and ultimately empower you to guide your organization with wisdom and confidence in the age of AI.

The Trust Question

"At a healthcare board meeting, a CEO admired an AI pilot's success, then asked, 'How do we make our clinicians trust it?' In that moment, I realized AI readiness isn't about technology—it's about trust."

— Boardroom Reflection

Table of Contents

Dr. Farzana Chohan

Table of Contents

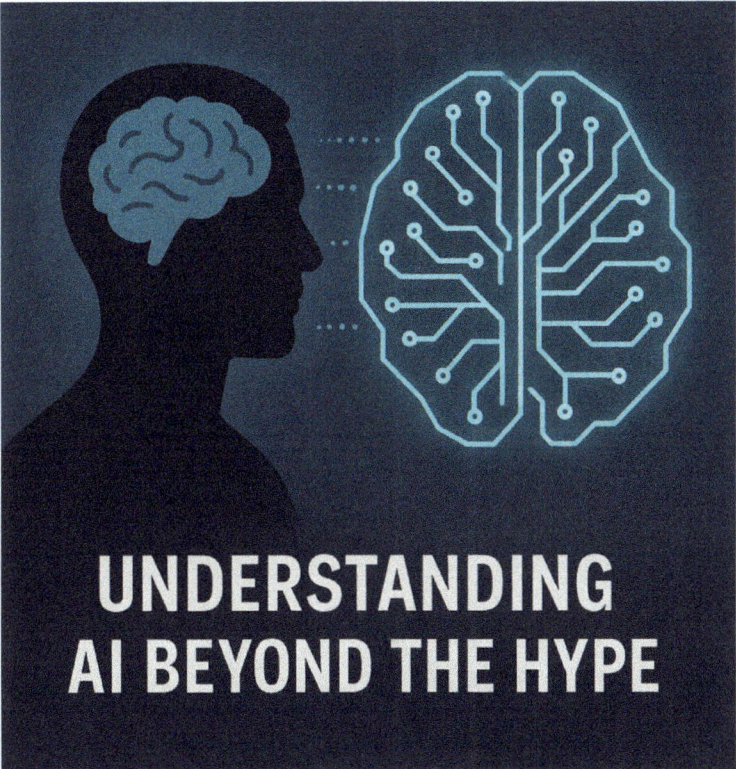

UNDERSTANDING
AI BEYOND THE HYPE

CHAPTER 1 – Understanding AI Beyond the Hype

As a healthcare architect, I once led a project designing a hospital's "smart surgery wing." We integrated sensors and analytics to optimize air flow, lighting, and patient recovery. The technology amazed us, but the nurses taught me the real lesson: data means nothing without empathy. When we adjusted the lighting based on their feedback—not just sensor readings—patient satisfaction soared. AI, like architecture, must start with the human blueprint.

To lead in the AI era, we first need clarity on **what AI is – and what it isn't**. Too often, discussions around artificial intelligence swing between overhyped dreams and dystopian fears. As a leader, your role is to cut through that noise and see AI for what it truly is: a powerful set of technologies that *augment* human intelligence, **not a magic brain that replaces it**. In simple terms, AI (Artificial Intelligence) refers to machines and software systems that can perform tasks normally requiring human intelligence – things like learning from data (machine learning), recognizing patterns, making decisions or predictions, and even generating content (as with today's generative AI models).

Let's break that down in plain language. **Machine learning** is the engine behind most modern AI – algorithms that improve at tasks as they are exposed to more data. Rather than being explicitly programmed with step-by-step instructions for every scenario, machine learning models *train* on historical examples to detect patterns and make inferences on new inputs. For example, by analyzing thousands of past customer transactions, a machine learning model can learn to predict which new transactions look fraudulent. **Generative AI**, a subset that has recently grabbed headlines, goes a step further – these models can create new content (text, images, designs) based on patterns learned from existing data. Tools like ChatGPT or image generators exemplify this ability to produce seemingly creative outputs. And then there's **automation**– using AI and software to handle routine, repetitive processes without human intervention.

Why do these distinctions matter for a leader? Because each carries different implications. **Automation** can yield efficiency gains – automating data entry or invoice processing, for instance – but by itself it often just speeds up existing workflows. **AI-driven innovation**, on the other hand, might unlock completely new ways of operating or new services (think of an AI system that analyzes medical images to detect diseases earlier than humans could). Understanding the difference helps you ask the right question: *Are we using AI merely to automate what we already do, or to innovate and do things we couldn't do before?* Both are valuable, but the latter is where transformative growth lies.

Perhaps most importantly, leaders need to understand that **AI is best thought of as "augmented intelligence" – a tool to amplify human capabilities**. AI systems excel at processing vast amounts of data, spotting patterns invisible to us, and performing narrow tasks at superhuman speed. But they lack the holistic judgment, empathy, creativity, and ethical reasoning that humans bring. The ideal approach is $HI \leftrightarrow AI$: a synergy between Human Intelligence and Artificial Intelligence. For example, an AI can sift through millions of network events to flag potential cybersecurity threats, while a human analyst vets those flags and makes nuanced decisions on how to respond. AI might draft a report or first-pass legal contract by collating information, but a human expert will refine it, add context, and ensure it aligns with strategic objectives. In short, **AI extends our reach and insight, but humans still steer the ship**.

To illustrate AI's augmenting power, consider a concrete example from healthcare: *OSF*

HealthCare's "Clare" virtual assistant. OSF, a hospital system, piloted an AI-driven chatbot to handle patient calls and inquiries. The results were striking – **within the first year, the AI assistant saved over $1.2 million in contact center costs and even generated an additional $1.2 million in annual patient revenue** by improving service and capturing appointments. The AI handled routine patient questions (like scheduling, FAQs, appointment reminders) 24/7, in turn freeing up human staff to focus on complex or critical patient needs. Rather than replace the human staff, it *augmented* them – mundane tasks were offloaded to AI, while nurses and representatives could devote more attention to high-value interactions requiring empathy or problem-solving. The hospital not only saved money, but patient satisfaction improved thanks to shorter wait times and around-the-clock responsiveness.

This case underscores a key point: **when AI takes over time-consuming but low-value tasks, humans are elevated to work at the top of their skillset.** In the OSF example, decisions that previously consumed staff hours (answering basic queries, routing calls) added little strategic value, but they ate into time that could be spent on direct patient care or process improvements. By deploying an AI for those tasks, the hospital's human talent could focus on what *does* add strategic value – patient outcomes and experience. Many organizations have similar opportunities. AI can comb through data in seconds rather than a team of analysts taking weeks, surface insights for managers to make faster decisions, draft routine reports or emails so people can concentrate on creative and analytical work. The question leaders should constantly ask is: *Which parts of our team's workload are rote, repetitive, or data-heavy – and could be accelerated or improved with AI?*

Reflection: *Think about your own day or your team's workflows. Which decisions or tasks routinely consume significant time but add little strategic value? Could an AI system assist with or even fully handle those tasks, allowing you and your team to focus on higher-impact activities?*

It's also critical to address what AI is *not*. Despite sci-fi portrayals, today's AI is not a sentient, all-knowing "robot overlord." It does not possess common sense or human-like understanding outside of narrow domains. A machine learning model is only as good as the data it's trained on and the objectives it's given. If the data is flawed or biased, the AI's outputs will be as well. If we ask the wrong question, we'll get the wrong answer faster than ever. Thus, adopting AI doesn't absolve leaders from thinking critically – in fact it requires *more* vigilance. We must verify AI-driven insights, monitor for errors or biases, and ensure the technology is truly serving our goals.

Finally, cutting through hype means being pragmatic about ROI. There's no doubt that AI can deliver impressive benefits – cost savings, faster service, increased revenue – but it often takes thoughtful pilot testing and iteration to capture those benefits. Throughout this book, we will highlight case studies (like OSF's) where AI pilots succeeded, as well as examples where hype outpaced reality. By understanding AI's capabilities and limitations, you as a leader will be equipped to champion AI initiatives grounded in real value, not just flash. In the next chapter, we'll introduce the AI Readiness Spectrum to help you assess where your organization stands in this journey from initial experimentation to strategic, transformative use of AI.

The Human Blueprint

"While designing a 'smart surgery wing,' sensors guided our data—but nurses guided our wisdom. When empathy joined the algorithm, patient satisfaction soared."
— Design Insight

The AI Readiness Spectrum™

	Strategy	Operations	People
Unaware			
Experimental			
Operational			
Strategic			
Transformative			

CHAPTER 2 – The AI Readiness Spectrum™

While advising a large operations team, we noticed their AI pilots were scattered—marketing had chatbots, HR had analytics, but no shared purpose. When we mapped their efforts, they realized they were "Operational" in pockets but "Unaware" in culture. Seeing it visually sparked action—they built a cross-functional AI council. Sometimes the mirror of measurement is what unlocks momentum.

How do you know if your organization is truly ready to harness AI? Some companies charge ahead with pilot projects but hit a wall when trying to scale. Others hesitate at the starting line, unsure where to begin. The **AI Readiness Spectrum™** is a diagnostic framework I developed to give leaders a clear, structured view of their organization's maturity in adopting AI. It breaks the journey into five stages **– Unaware, Experimental, Operational, Strategic, and Transformative –** across three domains: **Strategy, Operations,** and **People (Human)** readiness. This chapter will help you identify your current stage in each domain and provide a roadmap to advance to the next level.

Imagine a matrix with the five readiness stages as rows and the three domains as columns. We'll walk through each stage, but first, here's why each domain matters:

- **Strategic Readiness**: Do we have a clear vision and game plan for AI? Is leadership aligned on *why* and *where* we want to apply AI, tied to business goals? Strategic readiness means AI is not just an IT experiment; it's part of the organizational strategy (with executive sponsorship, funding, and defined objectives).

- **Operational Readiness**: Do we have the data, technology infrastructure, and processes to implement AI solutions effectively? This covers having quality data accessible, the right tools and platforms, and the workflow integration to actually use AI outputs in day-to-day operations.

- **Human Readiness** (People & Culture): Are our people aware of and open to AI? Do they have the skills (or training pathways) to work with AI? Does the culture encourage innovation, learning from experiments, and cross-functional collaboration on AI projects? Human readiness also includes trust and ethics – e.g., employees trusting the AI won't be used to simply cut jobs, and teams thinking about AI's ethical use.

The maturity *stages* provide a ladder of progress:

Stage 1: Unaware – This is the starting point where the organization has barely begun its AI journey. There's little to no understanding of AI's relevance or potential applications. No formal strategy exists, and leadership may not yet see AI as relevant to their business. In this stage, **Strategic readiness** is essentially zero (no AI strategy, and perhaps even a belief that "AI is just hype"). **Operationally**, there are no AI projects or supporting data infrastructure beyond standard IT. **People-wise**, employees and managers are largely unaware of AI beyond buzzwords; there may even be fear or misconceptions ("AI is sci-fi stuff" or "not for us"). *Key characteristics:* no defined AI initiatives, very limited knowledge or skills in AI, and possibly skepticism about its benefits.

Stage 2: Experimental – Here the organization has moved from ignorance to curiosity. There is **experimentation** underway, often in the form of a few ad-hoc pilot projects or proofs-of-concept. Strategically, the company hasn't fully committed – there may be isolated innovation teams or forward-thinking department heads trying out AI tools, but still no company-wide AI strategy. In the Operations domain, initial pilots might be running (for example, testing a chatbot in customer service, or using a machine learning tool in marketing analytics). However, these efforts are siloed; AI adoption is fragmented and not integrated into core processes yet. Data may be being gathered for pilots, but enterprise data governance or AI infrastructure is nascent. On the People side, awareness is growing. Maybe a few experts or external vendors are involved in the pilots, and some employees have attended AI webinars or training. But broadly, knowledge is uneven – some pockets of excitement, others still in the dark. The culture at this stage is one of tentative exploration: people are interested but also cautious, and there may be as much talk about AI as actual action. *Key characteristics:* one or more pilot projects, growing awareness of AI's potential, but lack of cohesive direction or widespread capability.

Stage 3: Operational – By this stage, the organization has learned from its experiments and starts integrating AI into core operations. **Strategic readiness** increases here; leadership has likely seen enough promise to formulate an initial AI strategy or include AI in the annual strategic plan. They set some goals (e.g., "Automate X process with AI by next year" or "Improve customer retention via AI insights"). **Operationally**, AI projects are moving into production use. For example, the pilot chatbot from Stage 2 might now be a fully deployed solution on the customer portal, or an AI-driven forecasting tool is used monthly by finance. There is investment in data infrastructure – perhaps a cloud data platform or new tools to pipeline data to AI models. The company might have established an AI or analytics team, or an internal Center of Excellence to support projects. Importantly, AI is yielding tangible improvements in efficiency, productivity or decision-making quality at this stage. On the **People** side, more employees have been trained on AI tools, or at least on data-driven practices. The culture is evolving to be more data-driven and tech-friendly. Some resistance may still exist (it always does), but there are also AI champions within teams. Middle managers are starting to trust AI outputs in their workflows, as they see time savings or better outcomes. *Key characteristics:* AI integrated into several core processes, metrics tracked for AI's impact, emerging governance of AI projects, growing internal expertise and comfort with AI.

Stage 4: Strategic – Now AI is no longer a series of isolated successes; it has become a strategic differentiator for the organization. At this stage, **Strategic readiness** means AI is embedded in the company's vision and competitive strategy. The executive team treats AI as crucial to staying ahead – similar to how companies treated going digital or adopting the internet in earlier eras. There is a clear AI roadmap aligned with business objectives (e.g., "Improve supply chain efficiency

AI READINESS FOR LEADERS

by 20% through AI optimization within 2 years" or "Launch 3 new AI-driven product features next year"). Leadership allocates significant budget and sets enterprise-wide KPIs for AI initiatives. **Operational readiness** in Stage 4 is characterized by enterprise-wide adoption. Multiple departments use AI systems; silos are broken down as data and insights flow across the organization. The infrastructure is robust – perhaps unified data lakes, ML platforms, and MLOps practices to continuously deploy and update models. Governance is in place to monitor performance, manage risks, and ensure compliance or ethical standards. For instance, a bank at this stage might have AI models in credit scoring, fraud detection, customer personalization – all managed under a governance framework for fairness and accountability. **People readiness** is markedly high: a large portion of employees have foundational AI literacy. There are training programs to continually upskill staff on new tools. The culture encourages experimentation and continuous learning; cross-functional teams collaborate on AI projects (e.g., domain experts working side by side with data scientists). Employees generally trust that AI is being used to augment their work, not simply to eliminate jobs – because leadership has been transparent and involved them in the transformation. The

30   Dr. Farzana Chohan

organization may even have an "AI ethics committee" or designated AI champions to foster responsible use (we'll explore this in Chapter 5). *Key characteristics:* AI woven into strategy and identity, enterprise-level coordination of AI, high data maturity, a learning culture, and proactive ethical governance.

Stage 5: Transformative – The pinnacle of the spectrum, Transformative readiness, is when an organization is *continuously redefining itself* and its industry through AI. At this stage, AI isn't just enhancing existing operations or strategies; it's enabling **new business models, revenue streams, or ways of delivering value** that were not possible before. Strategically, the organization views AI as a core driver of innovation and has the agility to pivot as AI technology evolves. They might even be *developing* AI technology themselves as a product or key intellectual property. For example, a manufacturer might evolve into a tech-enabled platform company by using AI throughout its supply chain and offering AI-driven services to partners. **Operationally**, an AI Transformative company has AI deeply embedded in every major process and decision. Real-time data streams and AI analyses guide daily operations at all levels. The company likely uses advanced AI techniques (like reinforcement learning or advanced robotics) and has a robust pipeline for moving cutting-edge AI from research into practice. Moreover, it continuously adapts processes as AI capabilities advance (a mindset of perpetual beta). **Human Readiness** in the transformative stage means the workforce is not only AI-proficient but AI-*fluent*. Employees have roles and workflows redesigned to maximize human-AI collaboration. A strong culture of *Purpose, Ethics, and Empathy* underpins the tech usage – the organization is acutely aware of the societal and ethical implications of its AI deployments and actively steers them by those values. Leaders here champion a vision of AI that elevates stakeholders and perhaps even contributes to societal good (for instance, open-sourcing certain AI tools or using AI for sustainability goals). *Key characteristics:* AI-driven innovation at the core of the business, rapid adaptation and learning, widespread AI literacy and comfort, active management of AI's ethical and social impact, and AI recognized as a key competitive advantage and competency of the organization.

To help you assess your organization, **Table 2.1** provides a condensed self-rating matrix. You can use it to score your Strategic, Operational, and Human readiness on a scale from 1 (Unaware) to 5 (Transformative). This kind of self-assessment can spark valuable discussions: maybe you're at a 3 in

Operations (some AI in use, moderate infrastructure) but only a 2 in People (skills lagging and cultural pushback). That gap would direct you to invest in training and change management. Or perhaps you're strong in strategy (vision is there, stage 4) but weak in operations (stage 2–3, experiments haven't scaled) – indicating a need to shore up data platforms or execution capabilities. The matrix template is provided below.

Table 2.1 – AI Readiness Spectrum™ Self-Assessment Matrix (Simplified)|

Readiness Domain	Stage 1 – Unaware	Stage 2 – Experimental	Stage 3 – Operational	Stage 4 – Strategic	Stage 5 – Transformative
Strategic (Vision & Alignment)	• No AI strategy • Leadership not engaged in AI	• Isolated pilot ideas • Following industry buzz, no coherent plan	• Emerging AI strategy tied to specific areas • Executives supportive; initial funding secured	• Clear AI strategy aligned to business goals • AI seen as strategic priority and regular board agenda item	• AI core to company vision and value proposition • Continuous strategy evolution with AI at the center
Operational (Data, Tech & Process)	• No AI projects • Data not prepared for AI use	• One-off pilots in silos • Ad-hoc data gathering for pilots	• Multiple AI use cases in production • Investments in data pipelines and integration begun	• Enterprise-wide AI integration • Unified data infrastructure & governance; MLOps emerging	• AI pervasive in operations • Real-time data and AI drive decisions; robust MLOps with continuous process optimization
People (Skills & Culture)	• Workforce largely unaware of AI • Fear or misconceptions common	• Growing awareness; pockets of enthusiasm • Minimal skills beyond pilot teams	• Workforce training underway for broader groups • Some specialists in-house; culture becoming data-driven	• Most employees AI-literate • Cross-functional AI teams; culture rewards innovation and learning; leaders champion AI ethics	• AI fluency organization-wide • Continuous upskilling; collaboration with AI embedded; high trust and ethical standards ingrained

Dr. Farzana Chohan

(Note: This matrix is a simplified guide. In practice, an organization might straddle stages – e.g., Operational readiness at Stage 3 while People readiness is at Stage 2. Use it to pinpoint weak links and prioritize actions.)

By filling out a matrix like this for your organization, you can visualize where you stand. It can be eye-opening. For example, a company might realize: "We have a strategic vision (Stage 4 in Strategy) and decent tech infrastructure (Stage 3 in Operations), but our people and culture are lagging (Stage 2) – no wonder our pilots aren't getting adopted!" That diagnosis then informs the solution: focus on change management, communication, and training to elevate the Human side. In contrast, another firm might see, "Our teams are eager and educated (People Stage 4), but we lack strategy and governance (Strategy Stage 2) – we need leadership to step up, define priorities, and invest in scaling what works."

Throughout the rest of this book, we will delve into each of these domains in detail: Chapter 3 on the human/leadership aspects (mirroring AI with human intelligence), Chapter 4 on culture, Chapter 5 on ethics (part of strategic and human readiness), Chapter 6 on moving from strategy to execution (operationalizing AI projects), Chapter 7 on upskilling people, Chapter 8 on measuring ROI (linking back to strategic goals), and Chapter 9 on the future of AI-augmented leadership (what Stage 5 looks like for leaders themselves). By the end, you should have both a clear picture of where you are on the AI Readiness Spectrum and a practical toolkit to progress toward the transformative end.

For now, consider discussing with your leadership team: *What stage do we think we're in today?* Don't be surprised if different people have different perceptions – part of the value is aligning on reality. And remember, there's no shame in being at an early stage; the shame would be staying there once you know how to advance. Every organization you admire for their AI prowess started at Unaware or Experimental not too long ago. With a map in hand, you can chart a faster, smoother journey to AI maturity. Next, we'll explore how human qualities – like purpose, empathy, and ethics – should mirror and guide your AI initiatives, ensuring that your path forward is not only effective but responsible and human-centered.

Seeing the Spectrum

"A Fortune 500 client realized they were 'Operational' in tech but 'Unaware' in culture. Mapping their readiness sparked a cross-functional AI council in weeks."
— *Advisory Experience*

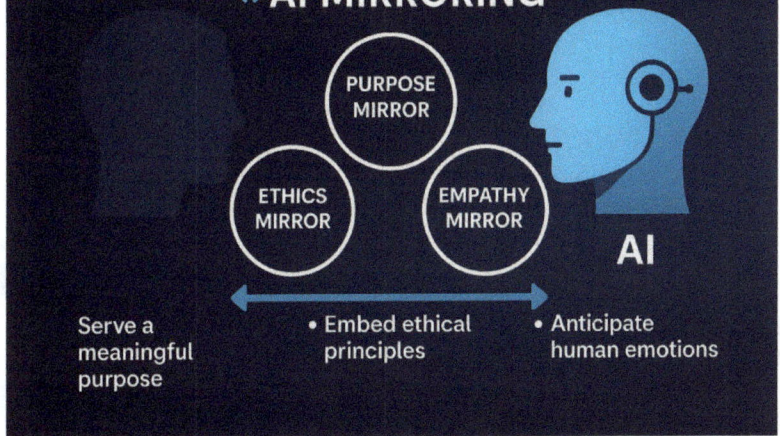

HUMAN INTELLIGENCE ↔ AI MIRRORING

PURPOSE MIRROR

ETHICS MIRROR

EMPATHY MIRROR

AI

Serve a meaningful purpose

• Embed ethical principles

• Anticipate human emotions

CHAPTER 3 – Human Intelligence Mirroring AI (HI ↔ AI)

After my Keynote talk on human-centric innovation, an audience member asked, "Can AI ever be ethical?" I asked audience, "what do they think, is it AI or it is AI's creator?" The response was, "Only if its creators are......" Later, in consulting with a hospital that used AI to predict patient readmissions, we saw this firsthand—the algorithm was powerful, but when we added empathy prompts for clinicians ("Call this patient to check if they can afford medication"), readmission rates dropped. That's HI ↔ AI in action—compassion coded into process.

At the heart of AI readiness lies a perhaps counterintuitive truth: *the more we integrate artificial intelligence, the more important our human intelligence becomes*. This chapter explores how uniquely human qualities – empathy, creativity, ethical judgment, purpose – must not only *survive* in an AI-driven organization, but actually *guide* the design and use of AI. We call this the **Purpose, Ethics, and Empathy Mirrors** framework. In essence, every time we deploy an AI system, we should see it as a mirror reflecting our human values. Are we building AI to serve a meaningful purpose? Are we encoding ethical principles into its functioning? Are we considering the end-user's emotional experience and need for empathy? By deliberately "mirroring" our best human traits in AI design, we ensure technology augments humanity rather than eroding it.

Why is this so critical? Because AI systems, left to their own devices, optimize for whatever we program them to optimize – which might be efficiency, profit, clicks, or other narrow metrics. If we don't infuse human-centered thinking, we risk creating outcomes that are technically optimal but humanly suboptimal. A classic example: A hospital might implement an AI scheduling system that maximizes operating room utilization (a pure efficiency metric). But if that system lacks empathy or context, it might end up scheduling a surgeon for 12 hours straight because it's "optimal" on paper – while ignoring the human need for rest, thus endangering patients and burning out staff. A human-centered approach would design the AI to incorporate factors like surgeon fatigue or patient anxiety, even if it means slightly less theoretical efficiency.

Consider the power of **empathy in AI design**. Empathy is the ability to understand and share the feelings of another. Now, AI itself doesn't "feel," but it can be designed in a way that takes into account human emotions and perspectives. As an illustration, imagine an AI-powered employee feedback analysis tool. A non-empathetic design might simply flag negative words in feedback and forward issues to HR. An empathetic design would consider tone, context, and provide managers with guidance on how to approach the conversation sensitively. Or take consumer AI: we've all interacted with automated phone systems that feel cold and frustrating. That's a design choice. If instead we design with empathy – anticipating user frustration, providing reassurance, offering easy opt-outs to a human agent – the AI interaction can actually feel more caring.

In fact, some of the biggest "AI failures" in the public eye have boiled down to a lack of human empathy and ethics in design. We've seen chatbot examples that turned toxic or biased because their training lacked ethical oversight. We've heard of facial recognition systems that misidentify people of color at alarming rates (more on bias in the next chapter) because their creators didn't ensure diverse, representative data. Each of these cases can be traced to humans failing to mirror ethical considerations in the AI. As one thought leader put it, the real problem often "isn't that our AI isn't smart enough – it's that it isn't kind enough". The algorithms may be highly sophisticated, but if they dispense decisions or information with zero regard for human impact, they *create harm*.

So how do we practically implement the Purpose-Ethics-Empathy framework? Let's break down each element:

- **Purpose Mirror:** For every AI project, ask "What human purpose does this serve?" This ties back to chapter 1's emphasis on meaningful innovation vs. gimmicks. If an AI doesn't clearly align to a purpose that people in your organization and your customers would care about, reconsider it. For example, deploying AI to speed up customer service is serving a purpose (better customer experience), whereas deploying AI because "our competitor did it" is not a purpose. Keeping purpose at the forefront also motivates teams and reduces fear – people see *why* the AI is being introduced and whom it benefits. One approach is to articulate a **"problem statement" or "opportunity statement"** for every AI initiative in human terms (e.g., "This AI will help our nurses spend more time with patients by automating paperwork," or "This AI will help customers get answers 24/7 so they're not left waiting."). Purpose acts as a North Star, guiding technical choices and reminding everyone that at the end of these algorithms are real human beings.

- **Ethics Mirror:** This is about consciously embedding ethical principles and fairness into

AI. We'll dive deeper in Chapter 5, but in short, it means considering issues of bias, transparency, and accountability from the get-go. For instance, if developing an AI hiring tool, the ethics mirror forces the question: *Could this unintentionally discriminate against certain groups?* (As Amazon discovered when its AI hiring model started downgrading résumés containing the word "women". An ethics check might involve steps like bias testing on your AI models, ensuring a diverse team is involved in development, and setting "red lines" for AI usage that align with your company's values. It also involves being transparent – with both employees and customers – about where and how AI is used, especially for decisions that affect them. If an AI is providing performance scores for employees or making customer recommendations, people should know there's an algorithm in the loop, and there should be recourse or human review for important decisions. At heart, the Ethics mirror is about maintaining trust. When employees and customers trust that your AI is being used responsibly and fairly, they are far more likely to embrace it.

- **Empathy Mirror:** Designing AI and surrounding processes with empathy means anticipating the human emotions involved and striving to make interactions positive or at least respectful. A great exercise for teams is to use *design thinking*, which starts with empathy: step into the shoes of the end-user or employee who will engage with the AI. How might they feel? What anxieties or needs might they have? For example, rolling out an AI tool that predicts which employees might leave (a "flight risk" predictor) could easily breed paranoia and distrust if handled bluntly ("the computer flagged you as a retention risk"). An empathetic approach would be far more confidential and supportive – perhaps the AI insights are only used at aggregate levels, or to quietly offer development opportunities to at-risk employees rather than singling them out. Another dimension of empathy is making AI systems *emotionally intelligent* in their communication. This doesn't mean the AI feigns human emotion, but rather it communicates with tact. Think of the difference in phrasing: an AI health app that says *"Alert: You failed to meet your exercise goal last week"* versus *"I noticed you had a busy week – it happens! Shall we set a small goal to get back on track?"*. The latter reflects empathetic design, acknowledging feelings and encouraging gently. Empathetically designed AI is not just "nice to have" – it can determine adoption. People will quickly abandon or work around AI that makes them feel dumb, guilty, or disrespected. They'll engage with AI that feels supportive or at least neutral and fair in tone.

The interplay of these elements can be seen in organizations that successfully humanize their AI. For instance, some banks implementing AI-powered customer service bots gave them a friendly persona *and* limited their authority – the bot would handle routine requests but automatically escalate sensitive issues to a human agent with an apology for any inconvenience. This showed empathy for frustrated customers and an ethical line that some decisions (like loan denials, fraud alerts) should involve humans. It also had purpose alignment: the bot's role was clearly to improve service, not to cut corners. Customers responded with higher satisfaction, and employees felt the technology was a partner rather than a threat.

Another real example: a global HR services company developed an AI tool to help identify employees who might need mental health support based on email sentiment and other data – a very sensitive area. They applied the Purpose-Ethics-Empathy lenses by (1) clearly defining the purpose as employee well-being and communicating that to staff, (2) building strict privacy and consent into the ethics (employees had to opt in, data was anonymized at certain stages, and any outreach was done carefully by human counselors), and (3) designing empathetic outreach messages that the AI would trigger (no one got an out-of-the-blue "the algorithm says you're depressed" email – instead, data quietly nudged a wellness representative to check in in a human way). The result was that employees actually *valued* the initiative – many voluntarily opted in because they trusted the intent and the approach. This shows how even in an area where AI could feel invasive, human-centric design turned it into a net positive.

In your own leadership context, fostering HI ↔ AI means encouraging your teams to not just ask "Can we automate this?" but also *"How should we automate this in line with our values?"* and *"How will people feel about it?"*. It means you as a leader role-model the integration of human judgment with AI insight. For example, if an AI report contradicts a long-held assumption, demonstrate *open-mindedness* (human curiosity) by investigating further, but also *wisdom* by not accepting algorithmic output as infallible. Say you use an AI tool for strategic planning that suggests a new market to enter – mirror human intelligence by questioning assumptions: *Did the AI account for post-pandemic trend shifts? Who vetted the training data?* – not to throw cold water, but to ensure alignment with real-world context and ethics.

In summary, **Human Intelligence mirroring AI** is about balance and guidance. AI can scale up information and options beyond what our brains could handle alone. But it's our human compass – our sense of purpose, ethics, and empathy – that must steer AI's application. When we get this right, the synergy is powerful: AI amplifies the best of HI (our strategic thinking, our creativity, our care for customers and employees). When we get it wrong, AI can amplify our worst biases or blind spots. Chapters 4 and 5 will continue this theme by examining how to build an organizational culture that embraces AI positively, and how to put in place the ethical guardrails so that trust and belonging are reinforced in the age of AI.

Coding Compassion

"When a hospital's AI predicted patient readmissions, we added a simple empathy step: a call to ask if patients could afford medication. Readmissions dropped. That's HI ↔ AI in action."

— Human-Centered Leadership Moment

CHAPTER 4 – Building an AI-Ready Culture

In one global organization I advised, the word "AI" triggered panic. Employees whispered, "It's here to replace us." So, we hosted open "Ask Me Anything About AI" sessions, where no question was too basic. One frontline worker said, "I finally get it—AI isn't replacing my job; it's helping me do it better." That cultural shift—from fear to curiosity—was the turning point. Productivity followed, but trust came first.

Culture eats strategy for breakfast – and that's true for AI strategy too. You can have a brilliant AI game plan and the latest technologies, but if your organizational culture is resistant or fearful, those initiatives will stall. Conversely, a supportive culture can accelerate AI adoption dramatically, as people find creative ways to make new tools work for them. This chapter focuses on how to cultivate a **culture that is AI-ready**: one that shifts the dominant mindset **from fear to curiosity**, from "this tech threatens me" to "this tech could help me," and that encourages learning, experimentation, and ethical considerations in everyday work.

From Fear to Curiosity: The Mindset Shift

It's natural for team members / employees (and leaders, for that matter) to feel uncertain or anxious about AI. Fear of change, fear of job loss, fear of failure with a new system – these are common reactions. An AI-ready culture doesn't pretend these fears don't exist; rather, it actively works to surface and address them, replacing fear with understanding and curiosity. **How?** Through open communication, education, and visible leadership support.

Communication is step one. Leaders should openly acknowledge both the opportunities and the anxieties around AI. Explain *why* the organization is exploring AI and *how* it will benefit not just the bottom line but employees, customers, or whoever the end-users are. For example, a leader might communicate: "We're piloting an AI tool to handle after-hours customer queries. This will relieve our on-call staff and improve response times – it's not about cutting jobs, it's about making your workloads saner and our customers happier." Encourage questions in town halls or team meetings. Make it safe for people to say "I don't get how this works" or "I'm worried about what this means for me." When people feel heard, their fear often diminishes because the unknown becomes knowable.

Education and exposure are the antidotes to fear. Often, fear of AI comes from not understanding it (it feels like a black box) or only hearing the hype ("it will do *everything*"). Providing training sessions, demos, or even simple explainers can demystify AI. Some companies run internal workshops or "AI fairs" where different teams showcase their AI experiments – employees can see AI in action and ask questions. The more hands-on experience people get, the more their mindset shifts to curiosity ("What else could we do with this?") instead of fear. It's also helpful to highlight positive use cases and quick wins. Sharing success stories – perhaps from other companies or from your own early pilots – can help employees see tangible benefits. *"At Company X, the AI scheduling tool gave everyone more predictable shifts. Let's see if we can achieve something similar,"* or *"Our marketing team's pilot AI campaign improved lead conversion by 15% – the team members are excited because it handled a lot of tedious A/B testing automatically."* Real examples turn AI from an abstract threat into a concrete tool with upside.

Leveraging **peer advocates and respected influencers inside your organization** can accelerate cultural buy-in. Identify the well-regarded employees who have embraced an AI pilot or who are tech-savvy and positive – enlist them as champions to informally coach others. People often learn best from peers. If Jane down the hall talks about how an AI tool helped reduce her reporting drudgery, her colleagues are more likely to give it a chance. Some firms establish an "AI ambassador" program across departments for this purpose.

The shift from fear to curiosity is also about framing. Instead of framing AI as *replacement*, frame it as *augmentation* (as we did in Chapter 1). Reinforce that the goal is not to make humans obsolete, but to relieve them of grunt work and enhance their abilities. And mean it – back that up by ensuring no immediate layoffs are tied to AI implementations, or by committing that displaced roles will be retrained for new opportunities in the organization. When employees believe leadership is sincere, they move out of self-preservation mode and into learning mode.

Surveying the cultural pulse can be a useful tool here. Some organizations deploy an "AI Culture Pulse Survey" to gauge how employees feel about AI initiatives – do they understand the strategy? Are they optimistic, neutral, or worried? We've included a template of such a survey in the Bonus Resources. The act of surveying sends a message that leadership cares about employee sentiments. And the results can highlight hotspots to address: for example, if the survey shows front-line staff are largely fearful, while R&D teams are excited, you might craft different communication strategies for each group or set up cross-functional chats where the excited folks can share their perspective with the anxious folks.

In summary, by communicating openly, educating, highlighting wins, and engaging influencers, you create fertile ground for curiosity. Employees start asking "How does this work? Could it help me with X task?" rather than silently dreading an unknown change. An anecdote from a client company: after a few months of deliberate culture work, an employee who initially said "They're bringing in this AI to watch over us and cut jobs" was overheard saying "I played around with the AI tool and found it could do this cool thing. I showed my team and we came up with an idea to use it in our next project!" That's the pivot from fear to curiosity in action.

Fostering a Learning and Experimentation Culture

An AI-ready culture is essentially a **learning culture**. It treats new technology not as a threat to the status quo, but as an opportunity to learn and improve. Leaders can foster this by encouraging experimentation (with guardrails) and making it "safe to fail" on pilot initiatives. If every failed experiment is punished, employees will stick to the old ways. But if *thoughtful* failures are treated as learning (and success stories are celebrated), people will engage more with AI.

One practice is to carve out time and space for innovation. Some companies allocate a few hours a week ("rotation days" or hackathon Fridays) for teams to tinker with new tools or data sets. Others run internal innovation challenges, inviting teams to propose AI ideas to solve business problems. These not only generate useful ideas, they signal to staff: we value your creativity with AI, not just rote execution of your current tasks.

Leadership behavior sets the tone. Are you, as a leader, openly learning as well? If you take an online AI for business course and mention it, or share an article you found enlightening, you normalize that it's okay not to know everything at first and that continual learning is part of the job. Managers who become "coaches" rather than taskmasters – supporting their teams in learning new skills – see far better adoption of innovations. It's powerful when an executive publicly thanks a team for an AI experiment *even if it didn't yield an immediate ROI*, because it provided insights or moved the company closer to a goal. That says: experimentation is welcome here.

Integrating Ethics and Trust into Culture
We touched on ethics in the last chapter and will expand in the next, but from a culture standpoint: **trust is the currency of an AI-ready culture**. People need to trust that AI tools are being

introduced in a fair, transparent way and that their concerns will be heard. If employees suspect AI is a clandestine "productivity monitoring" scheme or customers suspect AI decisions (like pricing or recommendations) are unfair, your cultural foundation cracks.

Building trust starts with **transparency**. When implementing AI, be clear about *how* it will be used and *what data* it will use. For example, if you plan to use AI to analyze sales call recordings for coaching, inform the sales team, let them know what the AI looks for, and allow them to see or verify its suggestions. Better yet, involve end-users in testing and giving feedback on the AI before full rollout. This co-creation builds trust and often improves the tool's design.

Another key cultural element is **appointing or empowering "AI Ethics Champions"**. Identify employees (or hire talent) who have knowledge or passion for the ethical implications of AI – perhaps someone in compliance, legal, or an experienced project manager with a keen sense of company values. Give them a mandate to be part of AI project teams to ask the hard questions ("Could this algorithm be biased? Do we have consent for this data use? Are we communicating this decision appropriately to customers?"). When staff see that ethics are taken seriously – even to the point of modifying or canceling an AI project because it doesn't meet your standards – it reinforces that *trust and values are not being sacrificed* for shiny tech. A striking statistic underscores this: in one study, **71% of employees said they trust their employer to deploy AI ethically if there is clear communication and demonstrated responsibility around AI use**. Trust blossoms when people know there are guardrails.

We must also weave **belonging and inclusion** into the cultural fabric. AI efforts should not be the province of an elite few; wherever possible, involve diverse voices. Not only does this mitigate bias, it helps everyone feel they have a stake in the AI journey. In team meetings, encourage discussions: "How could AI help our team?" This invites even those who are not tech experts to voice ideas (they often know the pain points best). When people see their input leading to an AI solution that helps them, it creates a virtuous cycle of engagement.

The AI Culture Pulse Survey Template

Included in the Bonus Resources is an **AI Culture Pulse Survey** template. Here, let's outline what such a survey might include and how you can use it:

- **Understanding & Awareness**: Questions to gauge if employees understand the company's AI vision and current projects. e.g., "I have a good understanding of how our company plans to use AI" (rate 1-5).

- **Attitudes & Emotions**: Questions about whether they feel excited, curious, anxious, threatened. e.g., "When I think about the impact of AI on my job, I feel: (a range from very anxious to very optimistic)".

- **Trust & Ethics**: Questions on trust in leadership regarding AI. e.g., "I trust that our leadership will use AI in ways that are fair to employees/customers" (agree/disagree scale).

- **Skills & Support**: Questions to see if they feel equipped. e.g., "I feel I have (or can develop) the skills to work effectively with AI tools" and "The company is providing the training needed to understand new AI tools" (agree/disagree).

- **Open Feedback**: A couple of open-ended questions like "What opportunities do you see for AI to help in your role or team?" and "Do you have any concerns about our use of AI that you'd like to share?"

Running this survey anonymously can provide a baseline and help tailor your culture-building actions. For example, if results show low understanding, that's a cue for more communication about the AI strategy. If they show high anxiety in a certain division, that might be a division to focus on with workshops or Q&A sessions. And importantly, share back a summary of results with the organization and what you plan to do about it. This closes the loop and builds further trust (people see you listened and acted).

Celebrating Wins and Normalizing Setbacks

To sustain an AI-ready culture, celebrate the *human* stories of success. When an employee acquires a new skill (like a marketer learning to use an AI analytics tool) and applies it to achieve a result, recognize that. When a cross-functional team runs a pilot, share their learnings with kudos for their initiative. These narratives reinforce the desired norms: that learning is valued, that using AI is a team effort, that it's the combination of people + AI that wins the day.

Likewise, handle setbacks with a learning-oriented tone. If an AI project doesn't deliver expected ROI at first, don't hide it or assign blame. Discuss it openly: *"Project Falcon didn't hit the 10% cost reduction target; we think the model needs retraining with more recent data and we underestimated the process changes needed. Here's what we learned and how we'll proceed."* This signals that imperfect outcomes are part of the journey, not a cause for panic. It encourages others to speak up about issues early (rather than sweeping under rug) and to persist through the improvement cycle.

In conclusion, an AI-ready culture is one of **curiosity, continuous learning, and trust**. It's a culture where employees feel they belong in the future vision, rather than being alienated by technology. They understand the *why* behind AI initiatives, they are given the *tools and training* to participate, and they trust leaders to consider *ethics and impact* on people, not just efficiency. In such a culture, when a new AI tool or idea comes along, the reflex is "Let's explore that," not "Here we go again" or "They're out to replace us." It takes deliberate effort to cultivate, but the payoff is huge: your organization can adapt faster, implement AI more effectively, and likely outperform others still mired in internal resistance.

As one CIO said, "Culture is the invisible hand that can either accelerate AI adoption or throttle it". By making that hand visible and guiding it – through communication, education, and ethical integration – you ensure it's pushing you forward. With culture on your side, we now turn to the next piece of the puzzle: ensuring our ethical compass is pointing true north as we scale up AI.

From Fear to Curiosity

"In one company, 'AI' meant panic. After open Q&A sessions, an employee said, 'It's not replacing us—it's helping us.' Trust grew first; productivity followed."
— Culture Reflection

THE ETHICAL COMPASS

FAIRNESS

ETHICS CHAMPION

CHECKLIST

ACCOUNTABILITY

DO THE RIGHT THING

BELONGING

ACCOUNTABILITY

PRIVACY

CHAPTER 5 – The Ethical Compass

Serving on an ethics committee for a tech-health partnership, we once reviewed an AI tool that detected early signs of depression from speech patterns. Brilliant science—but when we asked, "Did patients consent to this level of analysis?", the room went quiet. The rollout was paused until ethical safeguards were in place. The lesson: leadership sometimes means saying 'not yet'—because integrity travels faster than innovation.

In the rush to implement AI, it's easy to get caught up in technical capabilities and business gains, and lose sight of something fundamental: just because we *can* do something with AI doesn't always mean we *should*. **Ethical AI governance** isn't a buzzkill or a box-ticking exercise – it's our compass to ensure AI is used responsibly, fairly, and in line with our values. Leaders who make ethics a priority find it actually accelerates adoption (because people trust the systems) and yields higher-quality outcomes. This chapter demystifies ethical AI through real examples of pitfalls and best practices. We'll cover issues of bias, transparency, accountability, and belonging, and provide an **AI Ethics Checklist** along with guidance on establishing an **AI Ethics Champion** role in your organization.

Why Ethics Matter for AI (and for Business)

AI systems can unintentionally bake in and scale up biases or unfair practices present in their data or design. They can also make decisions that are opaque ("black box" models) and thus hard to explain to those affected. If left unchecked, these issues don't just pose moral problems; they become business problems – from PR disasters to legal liabilities to broken trust with customers and employees. Ethical lapses in AI have led to public backlash and even regulatory fines. Conversely, companies that champion ethical AI often strengthen their brand and stakeholder loyalty. People want to support organizations that use technology for good, not just for profit.

Let's illustrate the stakes with a few now-classic examples:

- In 2018, it emerged that **Amazon's experimental AI hiring tool was discriminating against women**. The model, trained on ten years of résumés (mostly from male applicants, reflecting the male-dominated tech industry), learned a bias: it down-ranked résumés containing words like "women's" (as in "women's soccer team," or women's college names). Amazon's engineers tried to correct it, but ultimately the tool was scrapped – they couldn't guarantee it wouldn't find new ways to proxy gender. The takeaway: If Amazon, with its tech prowess, could stumble into algorithmic bias, anyone can. The root cause was historical human bias in hiring; the AI merely mirrored and amplified it. An ethical AI approach would have caught this early: by testing the model for gender bias during development (an item on our checklist) and by ensuring diversity in the development team that might have anticipated the issue. Amazon's case became a cautionary tale – you don't want your company in that spotlight.

- **Facial recognition bias:** A landmark study known as "Gender Shades" found that some commercial facial recognition systems had error rates of <1% for identifying light-skinned men, but nearly 35% for dark-skinned women. In other words, these AI systems were far less accurate for women and people of color. This is an ethical and civil rights issue. Several wrongful arrests by law enforcement have since been linked to misidentification of Black individuals by facial recognition. For businesses, imagine deploying a face-recognition-based security or customer service tool that works inconsistently across demographics – that's not just bad PR, it could be outright illegal under equal treatment laws. The cause of this bias was skewed training data (the AI had seen many more images of white male faces). The fix involves more representative data, algorithmic adjustments, and sometimes deciding not to use face recognition at all in sensitive contexts until it's improved. The ethical principle is clear: AI systems must be evaluated for disparate impact. If they perform poorly for a subgroup or systematically disadvantage one, that's unacceptable – your ethical compass should point you to either improve the system or not use it in that manner.

- **Biased what-now?** It's not just hiring and face ID. Bias can creep in everywhere: loan approval algorithms denying certain zip codes due to proxying race/income (redlining by AI), medical AI systems under-diagnosing conditions in minorities because training data was mostly from white patients, content recommendation algorithms that amplify misinformation or polarizing content because it drives engagement. The patterns of historical injustice or skewed incentives can be codified in AI if we aren't vigilant. That's why ethical governance must be proactive, not reactive.

Core Principles: Fairness, Transparency, Accountability, Privacy, and Belonging

Let's break down a practical set of principles to guide AI development and deployment:

- **Fairness**: Strive for AI outcomes that are free of unjust bias and equitably beneficial. This doesn't mean you can guarantee absolute fairness in every sense (philosophers have long debates on what's "fair"), but at minimum your AI should not systematically disadvantage protected groups (race, gender, etc.) or other groups in unreasonable ways. Techniques: conduct bias audits. For any AI decision (hiring, credit, etc.), test outputs on different subgroups. If there's disparity, investigate and mitigate it before going live. Sometimes fairness might mean intentionally constraining the AI – e.g., not using certain sensitive attributes even if correlation exists, or adding algorithmic "fairness constraints" that adjust outputs to avoid bias.

- **Transparency**: This has two aspects. *Internal transparency* – your team should understand how an AI model makes decisions (at least broadly, if not every calculation) and what data it uses. Document the design decisions, the training data sources, and the known limitations. Then there's *External transparency* – being open with users or customers about the use of AI. For instance, if a customer is interacting with a chatbot, let them know it's AI (many companies now have disclaimers or name the bot accordingly). If an AI denies someone a loan or screens out a job application, ideally they should be informed an algorithm was involved and given some explanation. We might not always be able to provide a detailed rationale (AI can be complex), but even providing the main factors considered and an avenue for appeal or human review is crucial. Why? It builds trust and allows people to contest or correct potential errors. Regulatory trends (like the EU's AI regulations and GDPR's "right to explanation") are increasingly requiring this level of transparency for high-stakes AI decisions. Embracing transparency culturally also encourages better design; if a developer knows they may have to explain the model's decisions, they will likely design a simpler, more interpretable model or at least include explanation features.

- **Accountability**: Simply put, always have a clear answer to "Who is accountable for the outcomes of this AI system?" It should ultimately be a human (or humans) – whether it's the product owner, the department head, an AI oversight committee. This means you don't deflect blame to "the algorithm" if something goes wrong. If the AI scheduling system messes up employees' shifts, management should take accountability, apologize, fix it – not blame the computer. Setting up accountability also means defining escalation paths: when should a human be in the loop or approve an AI-driven decision? Responsible organizations often use a *tiered approach*: AI can automate low-impact decisions fully, but higher impact ones require human sign-off or at least a human fallback. For example, an AI can automatically flag 95% of low-risk loan approvals to go through but send edge cases or denials to a human loan officer for review. Accountability might also involve external audits: inviting a third party to assess your algorithms for bias or security. That might sound scary, but it can be a selling point – "We care enough to have independent audits of our AI."

- **Privacy**: AI thrives on data, but with great data comes great responsibility. Ensure your AI projects comply with data protection laws and respect user privacy beyond mere compliance. Use techniques like data anonymization, minimization (don't collect more than needed), and secure storage. If you're using personal data to train AI, consider whether you need consent. Data governance policies should extend to AI: how long do we keep model datasets? Who can access them? There have been incidents of AI models inadvertently memorizing sensitive data (like a language model spitting out someone's Social Security number because it was in training data). Guard against that by cleaning training data and possibly using privacy-preserving ML techniques where appropriate. From a cultural lens, make privacy a part of the conversation from day one of a project – not an afterthought. Encourage your team to ask: "This dataset has customer emails – should we really be using the full text of their messages to train the AI? What if there's personal info in there?" Often just raising the question leads to safer approaches (maybe extract only certain fields or get customer consent for using data to improve the service).

- **Belonging and Inclusion**: This principle is about ensuring that as you implement AI, you're not creating an environment of "haves and have-nots" or eroding the sense of belonging among your workforce or customer base. Involve a diverse set of employees in AI projects so that multiple perspectives are considered – this can surface ethical issues early and also helps everyone feel part of the change (not that change is happening *to* them). Also, think about how AI affects end-users of different backgrounds – for instance, if you introduce an AI-driven UX on your website, did you test it with users across ages, tech-savviness, abilities? Are instructions clear to non-native language speakers? Belonging in AI means the technology *works for everyone* and *everyone feels they can engage with it.* For internal use, watch out for morale issues: if, say, only a certain elite group gets AI tools that boost performance, and others are left behind, that breeds resentment. Democratize access as much as feasible, and frame AI as a tool for *team success*, not competition. Revisit Chapter 4's culture discussion: belonging is a key to performance and engagement, and how you roll out AI can either enhance or damage that. Strive for the former by being inclusive in planning and empathetic in implementation.

The AI Ethics Checklist & Champion Role

AI Ethics Checklist: Before deploying any significant AI system, run through a checklist such as:

1. **Objective Alignment** – Is the purpose of this AI system clear, legitimate, and aligned with our values? (Refer to the Purpose Mirror in Chapter 3.)

2. **Bias/Fairness Review** – Have we checked the training data for bias? Did we test outputs on different demographic or user segments? What mitigation is in place for any disparities found?

3. **Explainability** – Do we have an understanding of how the model makes decisions (even if approximate)? If a user or regulator asked for an explanation, could we provide something meaningful?

4. **Human Oversight** – Have we defined when and how humans can intervene? (E.g., a human can override the AI's decision, or AI only assists a human decision-maker rather than fully automating.)

5. **Accountability** – Who is responsible for monitoring this AI in production? Is there an "owner" for the system's outputs who will periodically review accuracy and impact? If something goes wrong, who responds?

6. **Privacy & Data** – Does this AI use personal data? If yes, are we in compliance with relevant laws (GDPR, etc.) and our own privacy policies? Are we minimizing data and protecting it? If using sensitive data (health, financial, etc.), do we have explicit consent or legal basis?

7. **Security** – Could the AI system be manipulated (e.g., adversarial attacks)? Are we safeguarding the model and data against breaches or abuse?

8. **User Consent and Awareness** – Are users aware when they are subject to an AI decision or interacting with AI? Do they have a choice or an alternative if they prefer a human interaction or review?

9. **Impact Assessment** – Have we considered potential negative impacts on stakeholders?

(This can be formal like an Algorithmic Impact Assessment.) For example, could this displace workers, and if so what's our plan to support them? Could it affect mental health (like an AI that filters content – what about the human moderators working with it)?

10.   **Continuous Monitoring** – What's our plan for monitoring the AI's performance and ethical compliance over time? (Metrics to watch, schedule for re-evaluation, etc.)

This checklist can be adapted to your context. The important thing is *not* to make it a mere formality. Engage relevant people in filling it out – the project manager, data scientist, business owner, maybe a compliance officer. Document the answers and decisions (this not only helps internal clarity but also would be invaluable if later audited). When an item raises a red flag, act on it: maybe it means delaying deployment to fix an issue, or adding a new control. For instance, if bias review finds the model is less accurate for a certain group, you might decide: until that's fixed, any cases involving that group get routed for manual review. Or if explainability is low but it's a scenario where explanation is needed (like credit decisions), you might choose a simpler model or a post-hoc explanation tool.

AI Ethics Champion/Committee: Depending on the size of your organization and AI endeavors, you may establish an **AI Ethics Committee** or assign **AI Ethics Champions**. A committee could be cross-functional – legal, HR, IT, data science, and business unit reps – meeting periodically to review major AI projects and policies. The champions are individuals, perhaps one per major project or department, who act as the ethical conscience and liaison. Their role is not to say "no" to everything, but to ask the tough questions and ensure the checklist and processes are followed. They should be empowered to escalate concerns to leadership if needed.

For example, a champion in HR might raise: "Our new AI-driven monitoring tool might erode trust, how do we ensure we use it transparently and fairly?" or a champion in product dev might say: "We need to include an accessibility review for this AI feature so it doesn't exclude users with disabilities." These champions ideally have some training in AI ethics (many companies now train their staff or bring in consultants for workshops). Encourage a culture where raising an ethical concern is seen as responsible, not obstructive. It's similar to safety culture in manufacturing – any worker can pull the cord to stop the line if they see a safety issue. Here, any team member can and should voice an ethical concern. That said, designated champions give clear ownership and expertise to the effort.

One real example: Microsoft established an AI ethics committee (AETHER) and later an Office of Responsible AI, with protocols and toolkits for teams. They famously created internal guidelines and even chose not to deploy certain AI capabilities (like facial recognition in some scenarios) until issues were resolved. Not every org is Microsoft, but the principle scales down: have a process to say "maybe we shouldn't do this," or "let's do it differently to be responsible." The **AI Ethics Champion** role description might include: facilitating ethical risk assessments, monitoring regulations, ensuring diverse perspectives in development, and being a point of contact for any employee or customer who has concerns about AI use.

Ethics and Belonging: Creating a Culture of Trust

Ethical AI governance isn't just an external mandate – it deeply affects internal culture and sense of belonging. When employees see that leadership cares about doing the right thing (not just doing the profitable thing), it builds a *purpose-driven culture*. People feel prouder to work there, which increases engagement and retention. In contrast, if employees feel the company would do something creepy or harmful with AI if it could get away with it, that cynicism erodes morale and loyalty.

Thus, communicate ethical decisions. If, for instance, you decide to disable a feature because it posed privacy risks, share that story internally: *"We discovered our AI could potentially infringe on user privacy, so we're redesigning it. Protecting our users is priority."* These narratives reinforce the ethical compass organization-wide.

Belonging also ties to making sure no group feels alienated by AI introduction. For example, if one department (say customer service) is heavily impacted by an AI chatbot (maybe fewer calls to handle), engage them in planning for how roles will evolve; perhaps those staff can be upskilled to manage the chatbot or focus on higher-touch support. Show that the company cares about *their* well-being, not just efficiency. That sense of fair treatment and inclusion in planning is part of ethics too – the **ethics of how we implement AI affecting our people**. Respect and empathy (from Chapter 3) come into play: an ethical approach would never treat employees as expendable cogs in an AI rollout, but rather partners in it.

Finally, remember that **ethical AI is a journey, not a checkbox**. Your compass may need recalibration as new issues arise and society's expectations shift.

Dr. Farzana Chohan

The important part is having one – a compass – and actively using it. If you commit to that, your organization will not only avoid many potential pitfalls, but likely create better AI solutions. Responsible AI tends to be higher quality AI, because thinking through edge cases and impacts usually uncovers opportunities for improvement. It's a win-win: you do right by people, and you end up with a more robust, trusted product or decision-making process.

With the ethical groundwork laid, we can now shift to execution. The next chapter will guide you from strategy into action – how to build an AI Transformation Blueprint and bring these ideas to life in projects and pilots. Keep your ethical compass handy on that journey, and you'll navigate much more confidently.

Leading with 'Not Yet'
"An AI tool could detect depression from voice patterns— but consent was unclear. We paused the launch.
Sometimes leadership means saying 'not yet' to protect what's right."
— Ethics Insight

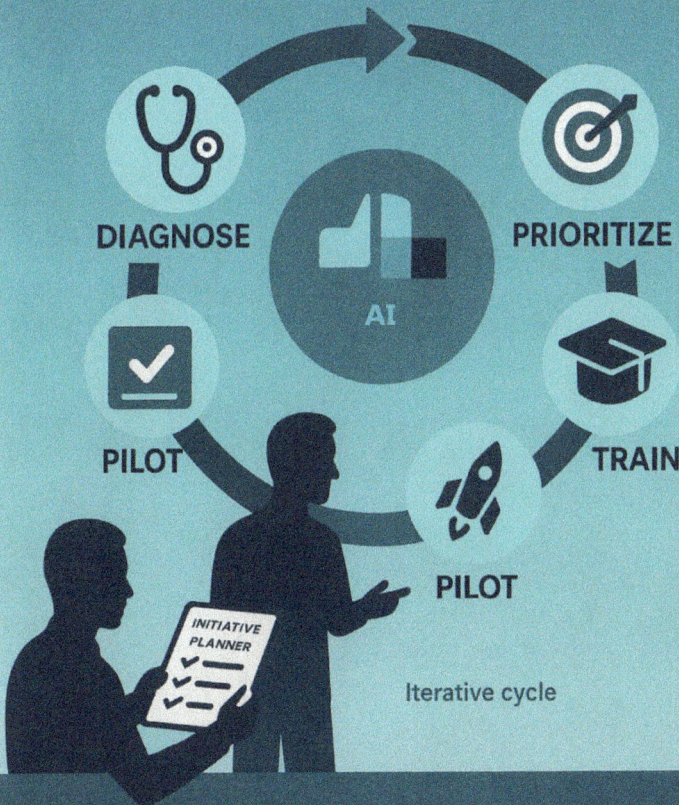

FROM STRATEGY TO EXECUTION

AI Transformation Blueprit

Diagnose → Prioritize → Define KPIs → Train → Pilot → Scale

DIAGNOSE

PRIORITIZE

AI

PILOT

TRAIN

PILOT

Iterative cycle

INITIATIVE PLANNER

AI Transformation Blueprit

CHAPTER 6 – From Strategy to Execution

In a hospital expansion project, the board pushed for an "AI-powered command center." Instead of starting with technology, we asked teams to sketch their ideal decision dashboard on paper—what information they actually needed. Those sketches became the blueprint for the AI system. Strategy moved to execution not through coding, but through clarity.

Up to this point, we've explored the *what* and *why* – understanding AI, assessing readiness, cultivating culture, and setting ethical guardrails. Now it's time to tackle the *how*: moving from high-level strategy to concrete execution. This chapter presents the **AI Transformation Blueprint**, a step-by-step approach leaders can use to turn AI aspirations into results. The blueprint consists of six key steps: **Diagnose, Prioritize, Define KPIs, Train, Pilot, Scale**. Think of it as an iterative cycle – you might go through multiple passes as you expand AI across the organization. We'll explain each step and include an **Initiative Planner template** to organize your AI projects methodically.

Step 1: Diagnose (Assess Current State and Opportunities)

Every journey starts with knowing where you are. In the context of AI execution, **Diagnose** means conducting a thorough assessment of processes, data, and pain points to identify where AI could add value. This step leverages a lot of the groundwork from earlier chapters:

- **Readiness Check**: Use insights from Chapter 2's AI Readiness Spectrum. What stage are different parts of the org at? This will inform how ambitious to be and where to focus first. For example, if your Operations readiness (data and tech) is low in most areas, your first AI projects might need to be modest and accompanied by foundational data work.

- **Pain Point Identification**: Talk to business unit leaders, process owners, frontline employees. What processes consume lots of time? Which decisions are often delayed due to analysis paralysis or lack of data? Where do errors frequently occur? Often the best AI opportunities lie in those pain points – places with repetitive tasks (ripe for automation) or complex decisions (ripe for AI decision support). For instance, a hospital might diagnose that scheduling ORs is a huge headache costing hours and creating delays – that's a clue to explore AI optimization for scheduling.

- **Data/App Inventory**: Catalog what data sources exist (and their quality), and what systems are in place. Maybe you find that you have thousands of customer support transcripts that could train a chatbot, or sensor data from equipment that's not yet analyzed. Conversely, you might find key data is missing or siloed, which you'll need to address. Diagnosing data readiness can save you from choosing an AI project that sounds good but lacks the necessary data fuel.

- **Benchmark the Industry**: See what peers or competitors are doing with AI. Sometimes an opportunity smacks you when you hear "Competitor X cut costs 20% using AI in procurement" or "Peer company Y is using AI to predict maintenance needs." While you shouldn't chase fads, industry trends can reveal low-hanging fruit or areas where you risk falling behind. If others in retail are using AI for personalized recommendations and you're not, diagnose why and whether you should prioritize catching up.

This diagnose phase might culminate in an **AI Opportunities Map** – a list of potential use cases or projects identified, along with some rough sense of feasibility and impact. For example: "Predictive maintenance for factory – potential high savings if downtime reduced, but data quality needs improvement" or "AI customer churn model – medium effort, data exists, could improve retention by focusing on at-risk clients." It's fine to cast a wide net initially.

One tool you might use is a **SWOT for AI** – looking at internal Strengths (e.g., we have a strong data science team, or lots of data in one domain), Weaknesses (lack of talent in some areas, legacy systems), Opportunities (areas identified as valuable AI use cases), Threats (competitors moving faster, potential disruption). This can help align AI focus with overall business context.

Also consider quick diagnostic wins: some firms do an "AI Readiness Workshop" or "Ideation session" with cross-functional teams to surface ideas and issues. You might bring in an external expert or consultant at this stage to get an outside perspective on where AI could be fruitfully applied – they might highlight something you missed (like using NLP to automate a report, etc).

By the end of Diagnose, you should have a clear picture of the landscape: a short list of promising AI project ideas, and knowledge of what enablers or blockers exist for each. Perhaps you'll realize some prerequisites – like needing to consolidate customer data before doing an AI CRM project – which then becomes part of your plan.

Step 2: Prioritize (Select Initiatives with High Value and Feasibility)

With a list of potential AI initiatives, the next step is **Prioritize** – decide where to focus first. Not all projects are equal. The goal is to find use cases that have a compelling combination of **impact, alignment, and achievability**. A common approach is to chart initiatives on a 2x2 matrix of *Value* (or expected benefit) vs *Feasibility* (or effort/complexity). You ideally pick the high value, high feasibility ones for early wins.

Key factors to consider when prioritizing:

- **Strategic Alignment**: Does this project clearly support a top business goal or solve a major pain point identified in strategy? Projects tied to revenue growth, cost reduction, customer satisfaction improvements, etc., typically get higher priority. Ensure there's an executive sponsor who cares about the outcome. Example: If your strategy is to improve customer experience, an AI that speeds up customer support aligns well and might outrank a back-office AI idea that's less strategic (even if useful).

- **Impact Potential**: Estimate (even roughly) the potential benefit. E.g., "If our forecasting AI improves accuracy by 5%, we could reduce inventory costs by $500k a year" or "An AI-powered personalization could increase e-commerce sales 10%." Some things can be quantified, others may be qualitative (better employee engagement, risk reduction). Rank projects by how significant their upside is. Focus on those likely to deliver meaningful ROI or competitive advantage.

- **Feasibility**: How hard is it to do this successfully? Consider data readiness (do we have enough quality data?), technical complexity (is the AI relatively straightforward like regression or very cutting-edge?), and resource availability (do we have or can we get the expertise?). Also timeline – can this deliver value in a reasonable time frame? Sometimes it's worth doing a harder long-term project, but you might balance your portfolio with some easier short-term wins. Use a **feasibility score** combining these factors. If a project has huge potential but would take 2 years of data cleaning, maybe it's not Phase 1.

- **Risks and Dependencies**: Are there big ethical or change management risks? (If yes, maybe not the best for a first foray.) Does it depend on something else (like "we need to implement a new ERP system first") – if so, maybe that dependency project itself becomes a priority before the AI. For instance, if all your valuable data is locked in disparate systems, you might prioritize a data lake or integration layer project – not glamorous AI per se, but an enabler for future AI. In prioritization, sometimes the top item is "get our data infrastructure in shape" because without that nothing else flies. That's okay; sequence accordingly.

- **Quick Wins vs. Moonshots**: It's often recommended to have a **balanced AI project portfolio** – a couple of quick wins that build momentum and confidence, and maybe one or two more ambitious projects that could be game-changers if they pan out. Early on, lean towards quick wins (something you can pilot in a few months) to show success and learn. But also keep the moonshot in view or in parallel if you have capacity – e.g., a transformational AI-driven product offering might be a moonshot worth incubating even as you implement simpler internal AIs.

- **Resource & Team Fit**: Consider which project fits well with the team you can assemble. If you have an enthusiastic department head in finance who's savvy with analytics, then an AI for finance might have a higher chance of success due to strong leadership support. People make projects succeed, not just tech. So gauge interest and readiness of the business owner for each idea.

Ideally, choose projects with a **"pull"** from the business (they want it) rather than only a top-down "push."

After evaluating these factors, it can help to create an **Initiative Prioritization Table** listing each project idea with scores or High/Med/Low on value and feasibility, plus notes on alignment and risk. Then facilitate a discussion with your stakeholders or AI steering committee to select the top candidates. For example, you might decide:

1. Pilot a **Customer Service AI Chatbot** – high strategic alignment (improving customer experience), moderate effort (we have chat logs, vendor solutions exist), good quick win potential.

2. Develop a **Sales Lead Scoring AI** – medium alignment (supports revenue), high feasibility (data ready in CRM, in-house data scientist available), could show ROI by next quarter.

3. Plan for a **Predictive Maintenance AI** – high impact (could save millions in downtime), but lower immediate feasibility (needs IoT data consolidation). This might be a longer-term one to start laying groundwork (install sensors, collect data).

Dr. Farzana Chohan

4. Put **HR Resume Screening AI** on hold – maybe identified, but after ethical review concerns and lacking diverse hiring data, not a Phase 1 priority.

And you might include a foundational task like "Implement Data Platform Upgrade – needed for multiple AIs."

Document these decisions in your **Initiative Planner** (we'll outline a template soon). Clear prioritization ensures focus. It's better to nail 2-3 key AI initiatives than to spread thin over 10 and not finish any. Remember, early success breeds support for later projects.

Step 3: Define KPIs (Metrics and Outcomes for Each Initiative)

With chosen initiatives, you need to define **Key Performance Indicators (KPIs)** and success criteria before jumping into development. This is crucial – it aligns expectations and allows you to measure ROI. As the saying goes, "What gets measured gets managed."

For each AI initiative, ask: *How will we know it's working? What specific metrics or outcomes will indicate success?* Define both **performance metrics** for the AI itself and **business metrics** that the AI is intended to influence.

Examples:

- For a Customer Service Chatbot: AI performance metrics might include **resolution rate** (what % of inquiries the bot handles without human handoff), **accuracy** of answers (maybe via customer feedback or QA sampling), and **response time**. Business metrics could be **average customer wait time** (expected to drop), **customer satisfaction score (CSAT)**, and possibly **support cost per contact**. You might set targets like "Bot to handle 50% of chats with CSAT equal to human agents within 6 months" – that's a clear KPI-driven goal.

- For a Sales Lead Scoring AI: AI metrics – **model precision/recall** (how well it predicts leads that convert), **lift over random**. Business metrics – **conversion rate of leads** (ideally goes up if sales focuses on high-score leads), **sales productivity** (maybe time to qualify leads goes down). A KPI might be "Increase lead conversion from 10% to 15% by using AI scores to prioritize follow-ups" or "Reduce time spent on low-probability leads by 30%".

- For Predictive Maintenance: AI metrics – **prediction accuracy** (how often it correctly predicts failures), **false alarm rate**. Business – **equipment uptime%, maintenance cost** or **downtime hours**. KPI: "Reduce unplanned downtime by 20% in the pilot plant within 1 year, saving an estimated $X in maintenance costs."

- For an Internal Process Automation AI: metrics could be **processing time per item** (expected to shrink), **error rate** (should reduce if AI is consistent), etc. Business impact might be **FTE hours saved** or **throughput increase**. E.g., "Automating invoice classification will save 100 hours/month and reduce errors by 90%."

It's important to establish a **baseline** for these metrics before AI implementation, so you can compare after. If average customer wait time is currently 2 minutes, and you aim for 1 minute with the bot, note that baseline. It sometimes takes effort to measure current performance (maybe you don't track something accurately now), but doing so is part of project prep.

Also, consider setting **stage-gate metrics** if it's a phased project. For example, "During pilot, we expect at least 70% accuracy from the model; if lower, we will retrain or reconsider approach." Or "We'll do a 3-month pilot in one region, and need to see at least $50k savings to justify scaling up." These pre-defined gates prevent the project from drifting without clear results – you know what success or failure looks like early.

KPIs also tie into our ethical and human considerations. Make sure you're measuring unintended consequences too. For instance, if you deploy an AI scheduling system to optimize shifts, a success KPI might be cost reduction, but you should also monitor **employee satisfaction or turnover** as a counterbalance, to ensure the AI's optimization isn't burning out staff or being perceived negatively. Similarly, for a hiring AI, beyond efficiency you'd track **diversity of hires** to ensure fairness isn't impacted. This reflects a holistic view of success.

Once KPIs are set, align with stakeholders: The business owner agrees these outcomes are valuable, the AI/tech team agrees they're measurable and realistic. This alignment is key; it ensures everyone knows what "done" or "win" means. Put these KPIs in the **Initiative Planner** for easy reference.

Step 4: Train (Upskill Team & Prepare Data/Tech)

Before or while you develop AI solutions, you often need to **train two things**: *the AI models* (technically training on data) and *the people* who will build/use them. Step 4 is about getting the necessary training done for both humans and machines, and setting up the technical environment.

On the human side:

- **Upskilling Pathways**: Refer back to Chapter 7 on Upskilling. Identify who needs what training for this initiative. For example, if you're implementing a new AI tool for marketing, your marketing analysts might need a crash course in using that tool's interface or interpreting AI-driven insights. If you're building a model in-house, maybe some junior data analysts could benefit from a specific course or mentoring on the modeling technique you'll use (like time-series forecasting or NLP). Plan for these in advance. Many organizations follow the 70-20-10 model here: formal training (10%) plus mentoring (20%) plus on-the-job practice (70%). Ensure the project team and users have time allocated to learn. It might be through online courses, vendor training sessions, or internally run workshops.

- **Cross-functional Training**: Sometimes success requires cross-pollination of knowledge. For instance, data scientists need to learn from ops experts about the context of the data (so they train the model correctly), and ops folks might need a basic understanding of what the AI does to trust and adopt it. Organize knowledge-sharing sessions. Even an informal lunch & learn where the data team explains the model in plain language to the operations team can build buy-in.

- **AI Ethics & Usage Training**: If deploying something like a chatbot, train the customer service team on how it works, how handoffs happen, and how to handle cases the bot escalates. Also clarify roles: the AI is not a "black box overlord" – it's a tool. Teach employees how to interpret and when to override AI recommendations. This training ensures AI augments humans rather than causing confusion or resentment. It may also involve setting guidelines (e.g., "If the AI's lead score is above 0.8, we prioritize that lead, but sales reps always apply judgment on approach").

On the technical side:

- **Data Preparation**: Likely a significant task. Clean the data, label it if needed, integrate sources. For a supervised learning model, you might need to assemble training datasets and perhaps do feature engineering. If data is messy or incomplete, maybe step 4 includes some process changes to start capturing data better going forward (e.g., ensuring support agents tag conversation topics so you have training labels for a helpdesk AI). This is where having data engineers involved is key. Sometimes it means deciding on a data platform or pipeline – e.g., setting up a cloud database to hold training data or installing necessary analytics software.

- **Infrastructure Setup**: Ensure you have the computing resources and software libraries for model training and deployment. That could be as simple as provisioning a server with a GPU in the cloud, or as involved as installing an ML ops framework or container environment for deploying the model. If using an external AI service/API, get the accounts and security in place. Essentially, make sure your "lab" is ready: the sandbox or environment where you'll develop the AI is secure and stable. Don't underestimate this – I've seen AI projects delayed because they spent weeks just getting firewall approvals or figuring out how to deploy code to production.

- **Model Development & Training**: This is the core technical work of building the AI. Data scientists/ML engineers will select algorithms (or use pre-built ones if using vendor solutions), then train models on historical data. They'll iterate, tune hyperparameters, etc. We won't detail ML theory here, but the important management point is to *track progress*. During training, the team should measure model performance on validation data (i.e., test accuracy, etc.). Make it a practice to compare against baseline (what did humans or the old method achieve?). For example, if manual forecasting was 70% accurate and the AI is now at 75%, that's improvement; track it. Also be prepared that initial models may not meet targets – then it's decide: improve via more data/features, try different model, or sometimes simplify expectations. This is why earlier we set stage-gate metrics: if after a certain effort the model is not hitting near a threshold, consider plan B (maybe a simpler analytics solution).

- **Validation & Ethics Checks**: As part of training, we must validate not just accuracy but biases or errors. If it's a customer-facing AI (like a chatbot or recommendation engine), pilot it internally or with a small user group to catch issues. For instance, test if the chatbot ever gives wrong or inappropriate answers. Have a diverse team test it (someone might notice something another doesn't). Validate against the ethics checklist in Chapter 5: e.g., if it's a loan model, ensure you test it on subpopulations for fairness metrics. This is in the training phase because it's easier to correct model or data issues now than after deployment.

One tip: maintain a **Project Playbook or journal** documenting what you did in this step – data sources, model versions tried, results. Not only is that good practice for reproducibility, it helps onboard others, and if leadership asks why you chose approach A vs B, you have a record. It's also essential if you later scale or transfer the project to another team.

By the end of Train (for the initial scope), you ideally have: (a) a working AI model or configured AI tool that meets performance criteria in a controlled setting, (b) a team that understands how to use and maintain it, and (c) data pipelines and infrastructure ready to deploy it reliably. Maybe you've run it in parallel with existing processes to see how it would have performed historically (this often builds confidence, e.g., "our AI would have flagged these 3 issues human inspectors missed – good sign").

Keep stakeholders in the loop through this. Small demos can be motivating – show the bot answering a real question, or show a dashboard of the model's predictions vs actuals to an exec. This maintains buy-in and perhaps solicits useful feedback early.

Step 5: Pilot (Implement on a Small Scale and Measure)

Armed with a trained model or AI system and an upskilled team, it's time to test it in the real world via a **Pilot**. Piloting means deploying the AI in a limited, controlled scope to validate its performance and impact under actual operating conditions, before fully scaling up. Think of it as a dress rehearsal or beta test.

Key aspects of a successful pilot:

- **Scope Definition**: Clearly define the boundaries. For example, "We will pilot the chatbot on our internal IT helpdesk for 2 months" or "The predictive maintenance AI will be tested on 2 out of 10 factory machines this quarter" or "Lead scoring will be used by the East Coast sales team only, as a trial." By limiting scope (to a region, a subset of users, a timeframe, etc.), you mitigate risk and make it easier to monitor. Pick a scope that's representative enough to learn from but small enough to contain any potential issues.

- **Baseline and A/B Testing**: During the pilot, you need to compare AI vs no-AI to measure benefits. If possible, run an A/B test: e.g., half of incoming support chats go to the bot first vs half go to regular queue, and compare outcomes. Or one sales team uses AI scores and another doesn't, for the pilot period, to see the difference in conversion. If A/B isn't feasible, at least compare to historical baseline as you go (e.g., downtime this quarter vs same quarter last year before AI, adjusting for any known factors). The key is to have a **control** or reference to attribute causation. Without that, you might attribute improvements to AI that actually came from something else (or vice versa).

- **Monitoring KPIs**: This is where the KPIs defined in Step 3 get measured in real operations. Set up dashboards or reports for key metrics. If your KPI was customer wait time, ensure your systems capture that in pilot and feed it to a dashboard. Many teams do a weekly (or even daily) check-in on pilot metrics. You might find initial results fluctuate as the system and people adjust. Give it a little time, but have a pulse on trends. Also monitor AI-specific metrics in production: does the model's accuracy hold up on new data? Are there more errors or exceptions than anticipated? Real-world often introduces new variables, so be vigilant.

- **Feedback Loops**: Collect qualitative feedback from users interacting with or affected by the AI. If it's customer-facing, gather customer feedback (surveys, interviews). If internal, talk to employees: "How is the lead scoring working for you? Do the scores seem to align with your gut? Any odd suggestions from the AI?" etc. Sometimes an AI can meet numeric targets but still have usability issues or unforeseen side effects that users can tell you about. For instance, maybe the chatbot works but agents find it doesn't transfer context well on handoff – that feedback is gold for improvement.

- **Iterate Quickly**: Use pilot learnings to refine the AI or process. Perhaps you discover the model is consistently underestimating something – you retrain it with new data including the pilot cases. Or users struggle with the interface – you tweak the UI or provide more training. Pilot is not just evaluation, it's improvement. Many successful AI deployments went through several pilot iterations until performance and acceptance were solid. Bake in time and budget for this tweaking. It could be minor (adjusting a threshold) or major (back to drawing board on algorithm). The point is to catch issues now. For example, one bank's fraud AI pilot found too many false positives at first – they iterated by adding new features to the model and improving data quality, and false alarms dropped significantly, making the solution viable to scale.

- **Manage Change**: During the pilot, treat change management seriously even though it's limited scope. Communicate to pilot participants about what's happening, why, and how it benefits them or the customers. Support them – if an employee in the pilot has to adapt their workflow with AI, ensure their manager is involved and supportive, maybe lighten other loads to give them time to learn. Recognize their effort – pilot folks are pioneers who may need to problem-solve on the fly. Highlight pilot successes to build wider organizational buy-in. For example, if the pilot yields a happy customer quote or a measurable efficiency gain, publicize that in internal comms or pilot review meetings.

- **Go/No-Go Criteria**: Before starting the pilot, have clear criteria for what outcomes would make you confident to scale vs needing more work vs maybe scrapping the project. It could be numeric thresholds for KPIs or qualitative gates (like "no major customer complaints"). At pilot end, hold a review against these criteria. If criteria met: plan scale-up. If partially met: decide if extending pilot or tweaking and re-piloting is warranted. If clearly not met and not fixable in reasonable time: possibly pivot or cancel the project (better to fail fast at pilot than after massive rollout). For instance, maybe the AI just didn't outperform humans as hoped; you either improve it or reallocate resources to higher yield projects – that's okay, that's why you pilot.

Document pilot results meticulously. This includes the metrics, feedback, changes made, and lessons learned. This documentation will inform scaling: you might make a "playbook" for scaling based on pilot (e.g., best practices discovered, pitfalls to avoid). It's also useful for knowledge sharing: other departments can learn from your pilot if they embark on similar projects.

One more thing: celebrate the pilot completion (especially if successful, but even if not, there were learnings). Thank the team and participants. This maintains enthusiasm and a culture that's not afraid to try new things.

Step 6: Scale (Integrate and Expand AI Solutions)

If the pilot is deemed successful (or after iterative cycles reach success), the final step is to **Scale** – roll out the AI solution at full scope to realize the broader benefits. Scaling is often where the real work of organizational change happens, and it should be approached systematically.

Key considerations for scaling:

- **Phased Rollout vs Big Bang**: Depending on context, you might still scale in stages. For example, after a regional pilot succeeded, you might roll out region by region, incorporating feedback as you go. This can reduce risk of overwhelming support teams or encountering surprises. Or if the pilot was comprehensive enough, you might flip the switch organization-wide. Choose what suits the risk level and complexity. A phased approach is usually safer, allowing mini-pilots at each expansion stage. It also helps manage workload (your AI team can support one region at a time).

- **Change Management at Scale**: You're now affecting more people (all users, all customers, etc.). Communication is crucial: announce the new AI-driven process or feature, explain its purpose and benefits, and how it will work, ideally leveraging success data from pilot ("In our test, resolution time improved by 30% with this new system, so we're excited to bring it to all of you"). Provide ample training materials and sessions for new users or those whose jobs change. Engage champions in each department (perhaps those who were in pilot can act as mentors to new adopters). And don't forget to communicate with customers if it's customer-facing. For instance, if rolling out a chatbot to all customers, maybe send an email or have a website banner: "We've introduced a new Virtual Assistant to serve you faster – here's how it can help." Setting proper expectations and framing it positively can drive adoption.

- **Integration into Workflows**: Scaling often means embedding the AI deeply into business processes. Ensure any process changes are documented and systems are integrated. For example, if previously a salesperson manually sorted leads, now ensure the CRM highlights the AI score prominently and maybe automates some steps based on it. If maintenance schedules are now set by AI, update SOPs (standard operating procedures) for maintenance teams accordingly. Align incentives if needed – e.g., update KPIs for staff to reflect usage of or outcomes from the AI tool (not punitively, but to reinforce the behaviors). Essentially, institutionalize the AI so it's part of the new normal.

- **IT and Infrastructure Scaling**: What worked for a pilot of limited scope might need hardening for full scale. Check that your infrastructure can handle increased load – more data, more users, more queries. This might involve optimizing code, adding servers, or subscribing to higher tier of a service. Plan for failover and redundancy if the AI becomes mission-critical. Also address security reviews for full deployment, especially if more data or external exposure is involved now. Work with IT and cybersecurity teams to ensure compliance and robustness.

- **Continued Monitoring and Governance**: When scaled, an AI solution should have an ongoing owner and monitoring plan. Set up automated alerts for key metrics drifting (e.g., if model accuracy drops or volume anomalies occur). The environment changes over time, so you might need a schedule for model retraining or validation (concept drift is real – e.g., consumer behavior changes, so a recommendation model might need retraining every X months). Have a process if the AI fails or needs to be overridden – people should know how to escalate issues. If an error happens at scale, handle it transparently and fix quickly (having that ethical/responsible mindset we discussed).

- **ROI Realization and Reporting**: Now that it's at scale, track the actual realized benefits and compare to what you projected. Are you seeing the cost savings or sales uplift as expected? If yes, celebrate and perhaps publicize (internally or even externally as a case study). If not, investigate why – sometimes projections were off or adoption is slower; you may need to make further adjustments. This is also where you can calculate ROI more solidly by comparing investments (time, money) vs returns achieved. Often initial ROI might be modest but grows as people fully adapt to the new system. Keep an eye on secondary effects too (e.g., maybe employee satisfaction went up because drudge work was automated – that's a win to report as well).

- **Scale the Learnings**: Beyond the specific project, consider how the lessons from this can be applied to other initiatives. Perhaps your organization now has a blueprint for AI deployment. Share that knowledge. This might formalize into an **AI Center of Excellence** if not already, where best practices are documented and disseminated. The success of one project can spawn ideas for others – encourage teams to consider where else similar approaches might apply. At the same time, ensure you don't overload by trying to scale too many things at once. But a strategic scaling could mean moving on to the next priority project in your roadmap, armed with confidence and experience.

- **Maintaining Culture and Ethics**: As the AI scales, continue to uphold the human-centric approach. Solicit feedback periodically even after rollout – sometimes issues appear later or improvements can be made as users become more sophisticated with the tool. Stay engaged with employee sentiments: do they trust it, do they feel more empowered? (this might be part of those AI pulse surveys or focus groups). Keep that ethical compass: monitor for any bias creep or misuse now that usage is broad. If you spot anything off, address it promptly and publicly – that reinforces culture.

By the end of Step 6, the AI transformation for that initiative should be fully embedded and delivering value. It doesn't end things – in fact, it's a new beginning of a "steady state" where continuous improvement and maintenance happen. But you can mark this as a milestone: you turned a strategic idea into operational reality, navigating all the challenges along the way. This is a huge leadership accomplishment and future-proofs a part of your organization.

The **Initiative Planner template** would capture each of these steps for each project. It might be structured like:

- **Project Name, Sponsor, Team**.
- **Diagnosis Summary** (pain point, baseline metrics, data readiness).
- **Priority/Alignment** (why we're doing this, expected impact).
- **KPIs** (list of success metrics and targets).
- **Training Needs** (team skill gaps and plan, data/model training needs).
- **Pilot Plan** (scope, timeline, responsibilities, criteria).
- **Pilot Results** (fill in after pilot – metrics achieved, feedback).
- **Scale Plan** (rollout approach, change management, monitoring plan).

- **Outcomes** (after scale – actual results vs target, ROI, lessons).

Such a document not only guides execution but serves as documentation for future reference or audits.

In conclusion of this chapter: moving from strategy to execution requires a disciplined approach, but by diagnosing properly, prioritizing wisely, defining clear goals, training people and models, piloting carefully, and then scaling deliberately, you greatly increase the odds of AI project success. Remember to be patient yet persistent – not everything will go perfectly in one shot. But leaders who shepherd their teams through this process will create tangible transformation and build organizational muscle to do it again and again. Next, we'll focus on the people aspect of that muscle: upskilling the workforce (Chapter 7) to thrive alongside AI, which is a crucial enabler for all we've discussed here.

Blueprint Before Code

"Before building an AI command center, I asked teams to sketch their ideal dashboard on paper. Those drawings—not the data—became the true blueprint."
— Execution Reflection

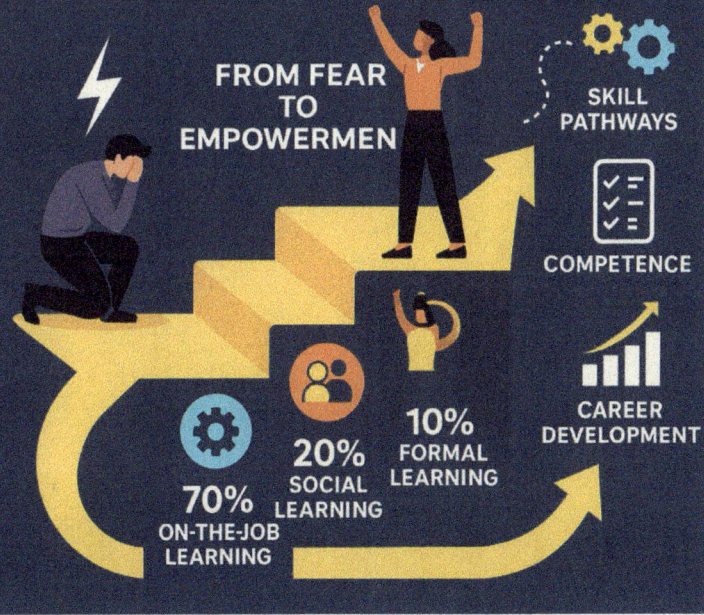

CHAPTER 7 – Upskilling the Workforce

When I led an executive workshop on AI literacy, one seasoned VP confessed, "I'm afraid my team knows more about AI than I do." I replied, "That's leadership— empower those who know." Six months later, he launched an internal "AI Buddies" program pairing data analysts with managers. The organization's readiness score jumped—and so did morale.

One of the most common fears about AI in organizations is, "Will it make my job irrelevant?" As leaders, we must address this head-on by helping our workforce evolve *with* AI. The narrative should not be AI *versus* employees, but AI *augmenting* employees – allowing them to take on higher-value work. To realize that, however, employees need new skills and a growth mindset. This chapter covers how to proactively upskill and reskill your people so they not only adapt to AI-driven changes, but actually embrace them as opportunities. We'll discuss structuring learning pathways (using the **70-20-10 model** and other techniques), specific skill sets to focus on, and how to alleviate workforce fears through competence and career development. In the end, an AI-ready organization is one where *human talent* has been elevated to work effectively alongside intelligent machines.

The Case for Upskilling: From Fear to Empowerment

As introduced earlier, a large portion of roles will be impacted by AI. The World Economic Forum estimates that **around 59% of workers will require significant reskilling by 2030** due to AI and automation. The worst approach a company can take is to ignore this until it's too late – or to treat employees as disposable, replacing them with new hires who have the needed skills. That fosters fear and disengagement. Instead, smart organizations invest in their people, building skills internally. This not only fills roles but engenders loyalty and harnesses invaluable institutional knowledge (tenured employees who learn AI can apply it with deep domain context).

We already see patterns: rather than AI eliminating jobs outright, it's changing the *tasks* within jobs. For example, a finance analyst might spend less time manually reconciling data (because AI automates it) and more time interpreting results and advising strategy. A marketer might rely on AI for basic copy drafting, but then focus more on creative strategy and campaign orchestration. So we need to shift worker skill sets up the value chain – more critical thinking, creativity, emotional intelligence, data interpretation, and oversight of AI outputs. Even roles like customer service: AI handles FAQs, so reps handle complex cases requiring empathy and problem-solving. They may also need to learn to *manage* AI – e.g., train the chatbot on new issues, or intervene seamlessly when AI transfers a customer.

Thus, upskilling is not just about teaching tech skills (though that's part of it), it's about cultivating *complementary* human skills and ensuring employees can use AI tools effectively (AI literacy). When done well, upskilling transforms fear into curiosity and empowerment. Employees start seeing AI as a tool in their toolbox rather than a threat to their livelihood.

70-20-10 Model for Continuous Learning

A practical framework to guide upskilling initiatives is the **70-20-10 model** of learning and development. It suggests that optimal learning comes 70% from *experiential, on-the-job practice*, 20% from *social learning* (coaching, mentoring, peer exchange), and 10% from *formal training* (courses, workshops). We can leverage this model for AI-related skill development:

- **10% Formal Training**: Start by offering structured learning experiences. This might include:

  o **Workshops & Courses**: For example, a workshop on "AI Basics for Business Professionals" to demystify AI concepts for non-tech staff. Or a course on using a specific AI tool (say, a training session on the new AI-driven CRM features for sales teams). There are plenty of online courses too – platforms like Coursera, LinkedIn Learning, or vendor-specific training (AWS, Microsoft etc.) for technical staff. Identify key groups and relevant curricula. For instance, data analysts might benefit from a course on machine learning methods or Python programming; HR staff might take a seminar on "AI in HR and ethics" to learn about algorithmic bias in hiring. Encourage participation and allot work time for it.

o **Certifications**: In some cases, pursuing certifications can structure learning. For example, certifying a few employees as "Data Science for Managers" or "AI Product Owner" etc., not because the paper matters but because the process ensures they've hit certain knowledge benchmarks.

o **Guest Speakers**: Bring in experts occasionally for talks or lunch-and-learns on AI trends, success stories, or even hands-on mini-projects. Hearing from an external thought leader can spark interest and new ideas.

Formal training sets the foundation, but by itself is not sufficient.

- **20% Social Learning**: This is where learning is reinforced through others:

  - **Mentorship & Cross-Pollination**: Pair up those who have more AI/data experience with those who don't. For example, you could have a mentorship program where a software engineer mentors a operations manager on data analytics basics, and in reverse the ops manager mentors the engineer on business context. Both learn. If you have a data science team, consider embedding them temporarily in business units ("fellows" programs) to help upskill those teams while the data scientists learn domain specifics.

  - **Communities of Practice**: Form internal networks or forums around AI topics. Maybe a monthly "AI in our business" roundtable where anyone can join to discuss and share knowledge or project updates. Encourage people to bring their questions and learn from colleagues' experiments. Some companies have "AI guilds" or internal meetups. For instance, "Citizen data scientists" from various departments can gather to swap tips on using analytics tools.

o **On-the-job coaching**: When rolling out an AI tool, use the train-the-trainer approach: early adopters or pilot participants become coaches for the next wave. Supervisors should also be coached so they can support their teams. For example, if customer service reps are getting an AI assistant, have team leads thoroughly trained so they can provide day-to-day guidance and answer questions as reps start using it.

o **Hackathons or AI Innovation Challenges**: These social events can spur peer learning. Mixed teams from different departments tackle a small AI-related problem or come up with AI use cases. It's learning by doing, but in a fun group way (fits 20% and 70%). We've seen employees who had zero AI background get excited and learn basics just by participating in a well-facilitated hackathon where they paired with tech-savvy colleagues.

- **70% Experiential**: This is the most powerful part – learning by doing real work.

  - **Stretch Assignments**: Assign employees tasks that involve using AI or data more than they have before. For instance, ask a financial analyst to use a new forecasting model (with support) and incorporate it into their next report, or have a maintenance technician work with the data team to label equipment data for the predictive maintenance algorithm. These assignments should be challenging but achievable with effort; the stretch forces learning.

- **Pilot Projects**: Involvement in the AI pilots (Chapter 6) is huge experiential learning. Even those who aren't core developers – e.g., the sales rep in the lead scoring pilot learns by interacting with that system and seeing how it affects outcomes.

- **Job Rotation/Shadowing**: Let employees spend some time (a few weeks or a month) in roles that are more data/AI intensive to pick up those skills. E.g., a marketing person could rotate into the analytics team for a project, or a call center rep could shadow the chatbot training team to see how it works.

- **Everyday Use and Iteration**: Once an AI tool is deployed, encourage employees to really use it and give feedback. Using it daily will naturally build skill and comfort. Make sure they have the agency to experiment a bit (e.g., try different what-if analyses in a forecasting tool).

- **Project Ownership**: Identify interested individuals and give them a chance to lead an

AI-related project, even if small. Maybe an HR staffer who learned about automation could spearhead an initiative to automate a minor HR task. Real ownership accelerates learning out of necessity and pride.

Crucially, the company should create a *safe environment* for this learning. People might make mistakes while learning new tech – treat those as learning moments, not failures. Reward effort and progress, not just mastery. If someone takes initiative to learn a new skill, recognize that in performance reviews or at least verbally.

A reflection prompt leaders can pose: **Which roles in our organization could be significantly augmented by AI, and what new skills would those roles need?**. This can help target upskilling efforts. For example, if routine data entry in accounting will be automated, those clerks could be trained in more analysis or in overseeing automated outputs for accuracy (so data auditing skills). If marketing content creation gets AI assistance, marketers need skills in AI prompt crafting and creative direction to refine AI outputs.

Specific Skill Focus Areas

While each role will have different needs, some broad skill categories emerge as valuable in the AI-enabled workplace:

- **Data Literacy**: Not everyone needs to be a data scientist, but almost everyone should be comfortable reading and interpreting data outputs from AI systems. That includes understanding basic statistics (means, trends, what correlation vs causation is) and being able to ask critical questions of data. Training on data visualization tools or basic Excel analysis can boost confidence. A data-literate salesperson, for instance, can understand the lead score and maybe even question it if it seems off given other data – that kind of healthy skepticism combined with understanding is ideal.

- **AI/Tech Literacy**: Again, not coding necessarily, but understanding what AI can and can't do, key concepts like machine learning, algorithmic bias, etc. enough to use tools properly. If employees understand that AI models learn from historical data, they might better supply that data or identify when something unusual happens outside the model's training. Also, simple automation tools (like RPA - robotic process automation) might be something many non-engineers can learn to use to lighten their own workloads. There's a trend of "citizen automators" where employees build little bots for their tasks using user-friendly platforms. Empower those who want to do that.

- **Digital Collaboration Tools**: With AI often comes more digital workflows. Ensuring people are adept at the digital tools (from advanced spreadsheets to project management software to communication platforms integrated with AI) is key. No AI works in isolation; it's part of a tech ecosystem employees must navigate.

- **Human Skills Enhanced**: Emphasize developing the human skills that become even more important as AI handles rote work. These include:

  o *Critical thinking and decision-making*: evaluating AI recommendations, making judgment calls on exceptions.

  o *Creative thinking*: using AI as a springboard for ideas (e.g., an architect uses AI-generated design options but then applies her creativity to refine the aesthetic and function).

  o *Emotional intelligence and communication*: especially for roles shifting to more client interaction or team coordination. If AI writes the first draft, the employee might focus on tailoring the tone and messaging – that needs empathy and communication skill.

o *Problem-solving*: framing the right questions for AI to answer, and solving complex issues that AI flags but can't resolve.

o *Adaptability*: this is more a mindset than a skill, but it can be fostered by encouraging employees to engage in continuous learning and to be comfortable with trial and error.

One particular skill is **"knowing when to trust and when to question AI."** That's a nuanced skill combining domain knowledge with basic AI understanding. Encourage employees to treat AI outputs neither as gospel nor as useless, but something to compare against their knowledge and sanity-check. For example, a doctor using an AI diagnostic tool should take its suggestion seriously but still consider patient specifics and perhaps run additional tests if something doesn't add up. That balancing skill comes with both training and building confidence through use.

Career Pathways and Retaining Talent

Upskilling should tie into career development. Show your workforce the *path forward* in the age of AI: how their roles can evolve and even new roles that might emerge. For example, someone in manufacturing might become a "automation supervisor" rather than a manual operator – monitoring and improving robot and AI performance on the line. An administrative assistant might evolve into an "information manager" who oversees AI scheduling and does higher-level project coordination now that calendar and email triage are aided by AI. Providing clarity or examples of these new career trajectories helps employees see themselves in the future, rather than fearing obsolescence.

Also, consider formal programs like **apprenticeships or bootcamps** for new tech roles. If you need more data analysts or AI specialists, it might be easier to retrain a few interested current employees than hire all new ones (especially since they know your business). There are success stories of companies taking people from operations or customer service and training them to be junior data analysts or bot trainers. It often results in loyal, motivated employees because you invested in them.

Address the fear of job loss directly. Be honest but optimistic. If certain jobs will be phased out, say you will do everything to re-skill those people for other positions or at least be transparent well in advance. Actually doing so – via training and internal mobility – will earn huge trust. A survey might find, say, **55% of managers spending 8 hours a week on manual tasks**; if you automate some of that, you should concurrently train those managers to use that freed time for strategy, not just cut headcount. Emphasize that message: AI is here to free you from drudgery so you can contribute more meaningfully. Then follow through by giving them the tools and training to indeed contribute in new ways.

Encourage a culture of **"lifelong learning"**. As one BetterUp study showed, high belonging is linked to big performance gains and part of belonging is feeling valued and invested in. A company that actively develops its people sends the signal: "You belong here in the future, not just until the next tech comes." That drives engagement. Some companies even give a small learning budget or time per employee specifically to learn new skills of their choice, which can include AI-related ones.

Finally, measure and celebrate upskilling progress. Track how many employees have gone through training, how skills are improving (maybe assess via quizzes or practical evaluations), and highlight success stories: "After learning XYZ, Jane automated a report saving her team 5 hours a week – and she got promoted to Data Specialist." This validates the effort and shows tangible benefit, motivating others.

Reflection: *Which roles on my team could be more valuable with even a small dose of AI knowledge or data skills? What steps can I take this quarter to help* *one or two people gain those?.* Answering that might lead you to sign up an employee for a course or pair them with a mentor, a small action that can yield big dividends.

By systematically upskilling your workforce, you not only ease the implementation of AI but you unlock human potential that was previously tied up in routine tasks. Your organization becomes more agile, more innovative, and more engaged – truly ready for the AI era. With skilled people and robust processes, the next question leadership will ask is, "How do we measure the success of all this transformation?" That leads into Chapter 8, where we'll delve into measuring ROI and defining success metrics for AI initiatives at a macro level.

AI Buddies
"A VP feared his team knew more about AI than he did. We created an 'AI Buddies' program pairing analysts with managers. Skills rose—and so did morale."
— Workforce Insight

Measuring Success & ROI

CHAPTER 8 – Measuring Success & ROI

A board I served on once asked for proof that AI was "worth it." Instead of showing cost savings, I shared a story: a scheduling AI freed 12 nurses' hours weekly, which they used for patient mentoring. Turnover dropped by 18%. Sometimes the most valuable ROI is Return on Intention— the human impact you can measure in trust and time.

How do you know if your AI investments are paying off? As with any business initiative, measuring the impact of AI projects is crucial to validate the effort, refine your approach, and communicate value to stakeholders. However, measuring the return on AI can be tricky – some benefits are direct and tangible (e.g., cost savings), while others are indirect or qualitative (e.g., improved customer experience, better decision quality). This chapter will provide a framework for defining **success metrics for AI**, linking them to business outcomes, and tracking ROI (Return on Investment). We'll explore key performance indicators like time savings, cost reduction, quality improvement, compliance rates, and engagement levels, among others, and discuss techniques for isolating the effect of AI in your results. We'll also present a sample **ROI Dashboard Starter Template** that leaders can use to monitor AI initiatives at a portfolio level.

Defining Success Metrics for AI Initiatives

In Chapter 6, we covered setting KPIs for individual projects. Here, we zoom out a bit to categories of metrics that frequently matter when evaluating AI adoption:

- **Efficiency & Productivity Metrics:** These capture how much faster or more output you get with AI.

  o *Time Savings*: measure reduction in time to complete a task or process. For instance, if an AI scheduling system means managers spend 4 hours less per week on schedules, that's time saved (and can be monetized by labor cost).

  o *Throughput*: more units processed per hour, more cases handled per agent, etc. If an AI automation doubles the number of invoices one staffer can process in a day, that's a throughput gain.

  o *Cost Reduction*: often directly tied to the above. If previously a process took 5 people and now it takes 3 with AI assistance (with the two moved to other needed work, ideally), the cost for that process is reduced. Or if AI optimizes supply ordering leading to less waste, that's cost saved. One can measure cost before vs after, or measure specific reductions like "$X saved in overtime pay by better scheduling".

- **Quality & Accuracy Metrics:** Does AI improve the quality of outcomes or reduce errors?

  o *Error Rate*: e.g., transcription error rate dropped from 5% to 1% after introducing an AI transcription tool. Or customer order picking errors reduced by some factor with AI vision checking.

  o *Quality scores*: many domains have quality indices (like manufacturing defect rate, or service quality rating). See if AI has moved the needle (maybe fewer defects because predictive maintenance prevented equipment issues).

  o *Consistency*: harder to measure, but sometimes captured via variance. AI might deliver more consistent results (e.g., every customer gets the same quality answer vs human reps where skill varies).

  o *Compliance and Risk*: an AI might catch compliance issues that humans missed (e.g., flagging biased language in job descriptions). Metrics could be number of compliance violations or audit findings pre vs post, or risk incidents. A study might find, say, "AI-driven compliance monitoring improved adherence to policy from 85% to 98%". That's quality in governance.

- o *Customer Outcomes*: In healthcare, did an AI diagnosis tool improve patient outcomes (lower complication rates)? In finance, did an AI risk model reduce loan defaults? These are domain-specific quality outcomes.

- **Effectiveness & Performance Metrics:** Particularly for decision-support AI.

    - o *Decision Speed*: time to make a decision. E.g., credit loan approval time decreased from days to minutes with AI, improving business volume.

    - o *Success Rate*: e.g., sales conversion rate improved, or predictive model's catch rate of fraud increased (we catch more instances now).

    - o *Utilization*: sometimes measured as how often the AI's advice is used. For example, "doctors followed the AI's treatment recommendation in 70% of cases where it was deployed, indicating it was usually valuable." If utilization is low, maybe the AI isn't trusted or needed.

- **Engagement & Satisfaction Metrics:** These include both customer and employee aspects.

  - *Customer Satisfaction (CSAT/NPS)*: Are customers happier? For instance, "Net Promoter Score rose 5 points after we launched the AI-powered self-service portal" or CSAT for chatbot interactions vs old IVR system improved. Or maybe resolution times dropped, leading to better satisfaction.

  - *Employee Engagement*: Did freeing them from drudge tasks increase their job satisfaction or engagement scores? Some companies measure internal eNPS or run surveys; if AI reduces burnout, you might see upticks in these metrics. Also track retention rates if relevant (belonging and empowerment can reduce turnover by 50%).

  - *Adoption Rate*: For internal AI tools, what percentage of employees are actively using it, and how has that changed? If adoption is high, likely indicating usefulness and satisfaction. If not, that's telling too.

- **Innovation & Growth Metrics:** Harder to tie solely to AI, but possible:

- *Revenue Growth/Contribution*: e.g., "AI-driven personalization contributed an estimated $2M in incremental sales this quarter" (which you'd estimate by comparing targeted segments or A/B tests).

- *New Products or Services launched enabled by AI*: count of new offerings or features (like "launched 3 new AI-powered features in our app, leading to X new subscriptions").

- *Competitive metrics*: like market share changes, which might be partially attributed to AI capabilities if they improve customer value proposition (though many factors affect these).

- **ROI Calculation:** ROI is typically (Benefit - Cost) / Cost * 100%. To calculate, you need to quantify benefits (e.g., cost savings, additional revenue, risk avoidance savings) and total costs (development, licenses, training, ongoing maintenance).

  - *Benefit quantification*: direct savings (less labor hours, less downtime), direct revenue (more sales, upsells), and sometimes intangible valued in $ (like time to market improvements or brand value from being innovative). If AI prevented costly errors or fines, that avoidance can be counted (e.g., "reduced risk of $1M regulatory fine – we might apply some probability to that to be conservative").

- o *Cost side*: include initial investment (software, hardware, external vendors, internal staff time). Also include ongoing costs for using/maintaining AI. If you have baseline for those, compare to baseline cost of old process. For example, old manual process cost $500k/year in labor; new AI process costs $300k in labor + $50k in AI expenses = $350k, so $150k/year savings.

- o Many companies in 2025 see ROI numbers thrown around like "451% ROI over 5 years" from certain AI implementations. That implies benefit was 4.51 times the cost. To legitimize such numbers, detail what's included. For instance: initial cost $100k, 5-year net benefit $550k ($650k benefit - $100k cost) yields 550%.

- • **Time to Value**: How quickly the benefits are realized. This could be measured as payback period (time for benefits to cover cost). For example, "Payback period was 8 months for the chatbot investment." Or track timeline of metric improvements to see how quickly AI made an impact.

- **Scalability metrics:** If part of success is deploying across more units, track that – e.g., number of stores using the AI pricing system, or percentage of processes automated out of those eligible. This shows progression of scaling.

It's important to attribute improvements to AI as best as possible. That's why as mentioned earlier, using control groups or historical baselines carefully matters. For example, if sales went up 10% after AI but market demand was also rising, you'd ideally isolate the AI's contribution via A/B tests or regression analysis controlling for other factors. Or if employee productivity improved, was it because of the AI tool or something else like a new bonus policy? One might use techniques like difference-in-differences if you rolled out in phases, etc.

Set up a **Dashboard** that tracks these metrics for each AI initiative and in aggregate. A dashboard might have sections like:

- *Efficiency Gains*: e.g., tasks automated, hours saved (with monetary equivalence).

- *Quality Gains*: e.g., error rate down X%, customer satisfaction up Y points, etc.

- *Financial Impact*: e.g., cost saved vs target, revenue added vs target, ROI %.

Dr. Farzana Chohan

- *Adoption/Usage*: e.g., how many processes or users are using the AI, utilization rates.

- *Project Health*: e.g., number of models in production, any that require retraining (this is more operational metric for AI management).

This could be visualized monthly or quarterly. Perhaps a bar chart of total $ saved to date, a line chart of CSAT over time, a gauge of ROI vs goal, etc.

Also include qualitative success indicators or anecdotes in reports. For instance, an employee quote: "The AI scheduling tool gave me back hours of my week, and I can now focus on team training, which I believe improved our store's sales." Or a customer quote: "The virtual assistant was so quick and helpful, I'm impressed." These bring life to the numbers.

Continuous Improvement based on Metrics

Measuring is not just for bragging rights; it's for learning and improving. When you see a metric not hitting target, investigate why. Maybe the model's performance has drifted and needs updating. Maybe employees aren't fully utilizing a feature, so more training or UI improvements are needed. Or if some department is achieving bigger gains than another, find out what they're doing right and replicate it across others.

Similarly, if ROI is below expectation, was the expectation too high (adjust business case next time) or is something underperforming? Perhaps a promised cost reduction didn't materialize because people are still doing the old steps out of habit – a sign that more change management is required.

Keep a long-term view too. Some AI benefits compound or grow as adoption grows. For instance, the first year might see modest ROI but as the model improves with more data and everyone learns to trust it, year two yields bigger returns. So measure over time and show trends. That said, if something is not delivering and trending flat, have the courage to call it and redeploy resources elsewhere (or try a different approach). The metrics will help justify such decisions.

On the flip side, highlight wins. If an AI project exceeded ROI goals or delivered in an unexpected way, broadcast that internally (and maybe externally if it's a competitive differentiator or PR story). For instance, if **OSF HealthCare's AI assistant saved $1.2M in contact center costs plus $1.2M in new revenue**, that's a huge win to share and motivate other units to think of similar ideas. It also shows stakeholders that AI readiness efforts are tangibly paying off.

One can even gamify improvement: for example, put departments on a friendly competition on adoption or satisfaction improvement with AI tools – as long as metrics are meaningful and aligned, it can spur engagement.

Finally, integrate these AI metrics into your organizational performance reviews and strategy reviews. AI should not be separate; if you have an annual strategy scorecard, include an AI capability or benefit metric. This signals to the whole organization that AI-driven improvements are part of how success is defined now.

In conclusion, by diligently measuring what matters, you turn AI from a nebulous buzzword into a concrete contributor to the bottom line and mission. Metrics tell the story of how combining human and artificial intelligence yields real-world outcomes. They keep efforts accountable and celebrate progress. With evidence of success in hand, leaders can better secure future investments in AI and scale initiatives with confidence. This measurement discipline, paired with the human-centric strategies we've discussed, will prepare your organization to not just do AI projects, but to truly become an AI-augmented enterprise.

Next, in Chapter 9, we will look at the evolving role of leaders themselves in an AI-augmented world, profiling those who have successfully integrated AI into their leadership approach and how they map out augmenting their own capabilities and their teams'.

Return on Intention

"An AI scheduler freed twelve nurses' hours each week. They used that time to mentor patients—and turnover fell by 18%. Sometimes ROI means Return on Intention."
— Impact Reflection

AI-AUGMENTED LEADERSHIP

CHAPTER 9 – The Future of AI-Augmented Leadership

In an executive retreat, a peer asked me, "What will define great leaders ten years from now?" I said, "Those who are humble enough to learn from AI, and wise enough to remain human." The room went quiet. The AI era doesn't demand superhumans—it demands self-aware humans.

As we integrate AI into our organizations, a vital question arises: *What does leadership look like in this new era?* The core principles of good leadership – vision, empathy, integrity, decisiveness – remain unchanged, but the context in which leaders operate is shifting rapidly. The leaders of the future (indeed, of the present) are those who can effectively partner with AI, leveraging it to enhance their decision-making, inclusivity, and impact. In this chapter, we profile the traits and practices of **adaptive, inclusive leaders** who have embraced AI as a collaborator rather than a mere tool. These leaders use AI to inform their strategies but still exercise uniquely human judgment where it counts. We will also introduce a **Leadership Augmentation Map** exercise that you as a leader (and your leadership team) can perform to identify areas where AI can augment your capabilities and where you, in turn, must amplify the human elements.

Profiles of AI-Augmented Leaders

Let's consider a few composite (but reality-inspired) portraits of AI-empowered leadership:

1. The Data-Driven Decision Maker (with Heart): This executive, say a COO of a retail chain, has cultivated a habit of grounding decisions in data, often using AI analytics platforms. For example, when deciding store staffing or inventory levels, they consult AI forecasts and simulations. However, they don't do so blindly. They ask their team critical questions about the AI's recommendations (How was this forecast derived? Is anything not captured?). They combine the AI's insight with their frontline managers' on-the-ground knowledge – balancing quantitative and qualitative factors. This leader might have weekly "AI briefings" where an internal data science team presents key trends or anomalies spotted by AI, which the leader then discusses with regional managers to contextualize. The result: faster decisions that are usually right but also buy-in from people because the leader involves them and applies common sense. Such a leader shows that being data-driven doesn't mean being cold or detached; it's about **augmenting intuition with**

information. They build trust in AI by being transparent about when they're using it and by crediting it for successes (e.g., "Our AI model helped spot a shift in customer preference early, which, combined with our team's rapid response, boosted sales 10%"). Yet, if the AI flags something that contradicts the company's core values or mission, this leader will probe further – for instance, an AI might suggest cost cuts that hurt employee morale; the leader might decline that route, showing human judgment ultimately steers the ship.

2. The Empathetic Innovator: Imagine a Chief Human Resources Officer who oversees hiring, training, and culture in a company using AI in HR processes. This CHRO implemented an AI-driven talent sourcing tool that significantly sped up identifying candidates, but they were very aware of potential bias. They convened a diverse committee to review the AI's recommendations for fairness. They also use AI sentiment analysis on employee surveys to gauge morale continuously. But what makes them stand out is how they act on that data. For example, AI might reveal subtle signs of burnout in a certain department (via analysis of feedback and maybe even meeting load metrics). This leader responds with a very human touch: personally meeting with that team's manager, organizing listening sessions, and implementing changes like extra rest days or more support. Essentially, they use AI to *enhance empathy at scale* – picking up weak signals across a large organization that no individual could notice, and then doubling down on empathetic leadership interventions. Employees report feeling heard and valued, because this leader ensures that behind every AI insight, there is authentic human concern and action. This leader also champions ethical AI use as part of inclusive culture. They might say to the workforce, "We're using AI to help us be more attuned to your needs, not to micromanage you. Your feedback trains the AI, and your managers, including me, are here to listen and help." In doing so, they maintain trust and belonging even as AI tools are adopted widely.

3. The Inclusive Strategist: Consider a business unit general manager who has a diverse team and a complex operation to run. This leader uses AI tools to democratize insight and involve team members in strategy. For instance, they set up a dashboard accessible to all team leads that uses AI to project project timelines, budget statuses, and risks. In weekly meetings, junior analysts are empowered to speak up about what the AI is showing because the leader explicitly asks them, "What are our data telling us this week? Anyone see something noteworthy?" This inclusive approach means decisions are enriched by many perspectives interpreting the AI outputs, not just the leader's interpretation. In one case, a team member might notice the AI forecast doesn't account for a market trend they're aware of; the leader encourages exploring that – maybe adjusting the model or complementing it with another analysis. This leader is not threatened by an AI knowing more about certain details than they do; instead, they relish it because it frees them to focus on big-picture and coaching. They might say, "The AI has the numbers for us, so let's talk about how we respond creatively and collaboratively." They also ensure AI tools are accessible and understandable to all – if someone on the team doesn't get how a prediction was made, this leader will have the data science team explain it in lay terms. This fosters an inclusive environment where no one feels left behind by technology, and everyone is invited to upskill and contribute. As a result, their unit is agile – they spot opportunities or issues sooner and align on strategy faster because AI provided a common reference point grounded in data.

4. The Ethical Guardian with Vision: Picture a CEO who is very bullish on integrating AI into products and operations, but equally vocal about doing it responsibly. This CEO establishes an AI ethics board (including external advisors) to review major AI deployments, and personally attends those meetings sometimes to underscore importance. When a conflict arises – say an AI feature could boost profits but has privacy trade-offs – they weigh it carefully, openly, and often choose the route that maintains trust and brand integrity even if it means slower short-term growth. That stance actually pays off long-term because customers and regulators see the company as trustworthy. This leader also articulates an inspiring vision of how AI and humanity together can achieve the company's purpose. For example, they might express: "AI is going to handle the mundane so our talented people can focus on innovation and customer relationships – that's where we shine as humans." Under their leadership, stories of human-AI collaboration successes are celebrated: e.g., how an engineer worked with an AI design tool to create a breakthrough product. They set a tone that AI use should always align with core values (like fairness, transparency, quality). This CEO doesn't necessarily code or understand the math deeply, but they ask the right questions, push for clarity ("Explain to me how this algorithm makes decisions in customer terms"), and ensure a culture where raising concerns about AI is encouraged, not stifled. Their combination of visionary excitement and principled caution serves as a model for industry peers.

From these profiles, we see patterns of **AI-augmented leaders**: they use data for informed decisions but keep human judgment at the helm; they enhance their empathy and inclusivity through AI tools; they spread AI literacy and involve others; and they stand firm on ethics and values, setting guardrails for AI usage. In doing so, they amplify both their **analytical intelligence** and their **emotional intelligence**.

The Leadership Augmentation Map

To guide your own development as an AI-era leader, an exercise is to create a **Leadership Augmentation Map**. This is a simple two-column or quadrant exercise:

On one side, list key leadership activities or competencies you have (or need). Examples: strategic planning, decision-making under uncertainty, communicating vision, mentoring staff, crisis management, innovation, network building, etc.

For each, ask:

- How could AI/data tools augment or support me in this area?

- What uniquely human strengths do I need to double down on that AI can't replace here?

Fill in ideas:

- For strategic planning: AI can provide forecasting and scenario modeling to give you a clearer picture of possible futures (so use those to test your strategy). It can also aggregate market intelligence (like analyzing thousands of articles or social media sentiments) to inform your view. But the human part is creativity and vision – AI won't set your vision for you; it only informs it. So you might note: *Use AI trend analysis quarterly to challenge/refine strategic assumptions; spend saved time on cultivating stakeholder alignment around the refined vision.* That way AI augments data analysis, and you focus on inspiring people with the vision.

- For decision-making: If you face, say, resource allocation decisions, you could use AI optimization to suggest allocations. But human judgment will incorporate ethical considerations and tacit knowledge. Note: *AI will crunch the numbers on ROI for projects; I will weigh alignment with mission and moral implications that numbers don't capture.* For uncertain decisions, maybe you use AI to simulate outcomes, but then trust your gut on things like team morale impact.

- For communication: Perhaps AI tools can help draft initial versions of presentations or emails (some leaders already use GPT-like tools for speech drafts). Note: *Use AI to draft data-heavy parts of communication so I can focus on the emotional and storytelling aspects.* Then you polish with personal anecdotes and authentic tone that AI can't emulate well.

- For mentoring/coaching: AI might help track team performance metrics, highlight who might need help (like if someone's productivity drops or learning progress stalls). But empathy and tailored advice are human. Note: *Review AI-curated dashboard of team KPIs weekly to spot who might need coaching; then devote time to one-on-ones with deep listening and guidance.* Here AI augments awareness, you bring the human connection.

- For innovation: AI can generate lots of ideas or designs (e.g., via generative design tools) beyond human brain capacity. Use that to widen the solution space. But creative judgment to pick and refine ideas remains human. Note: *Run AI brainstorming with team for concept ideas; then facilitate human workshop to evaluate and build on the best ideas, using intuition and customer empathy.*

- For crisis management: AI could provide real-time data and predictive insights in a crisis (like supply chain disruption). But trust-building, calm leadership presence, and tough value-based decisions (like taking a short-term hit to protect long-term brand) are on you. Note: *Leverage AI early warning systems for crises; uphold human values (transparency, decisiveness with compassion) in responding to crises.*

- Network building: AI can analyze your network or suggest who to connect with (like LinkedIn suggestions, etc.). But genuine relationship building is human domain. Note: *Use AI to identify potential mentors/partners globally; initiate contact personally and nurture with human interaction (calls, personal notes).*

By mapping these out, you essentially draw a blueprint of your future leadership model:

- You identify tools or practices to adopt: e.g., get training on that forecasting software, or subscribe to that AI analytics feed.

- You identify skills to strengthen in yourself: perhaps you realize you need to improve storytelling ability since data alone won't sway people; or increase emotional intelligence to complement all the data flying around.

Dr. Farzana Chohan

- You also identify outdated habits to drop: maybe you currently spend hours crunching numbers for planning – something an analyst + AI can do, freeing you to do more leading and less number-crunching. So you plan to delegate and automate more.

This map can be revisited periodically. It's akin to personal agility – as AI tools evolve, you'll integrate new ones and shift your human focus accordingly. Maybe in 3 years, AI could handle even more of a certain area, prompting you to lean even further into creative or relational tasks.

It can be helpful to share such maps among your leadership team too, to align on how roles might change and support each other in that growth. Some might be early adopters who can mentor others in using AI. The CFO could help others understand AI analytics, the HR head could guide on the human aspects, etc.

The end-goal is a leadership team comfortable with AI as a colleague – one that uses AI for its strengths (data processing, pattern finding, optimization) and themselves for human strengths (vision, empathy, ethics, inspiration). These leaders don't fear being replaced because they continuously redefine their roles to focus on what humans do best. They ensure they are the leaders who use AI to replace those who do not, as the old adage goes.

As you become such a leader, you also set the tone for your organization. Leaders model behavior – if you openly use AI tools and discuss their outputs thoughtfully, your team will be encouraged to do the same. If you also demonstrate where you override AI with human judgment (and explain why), you teach a critical thinking approach. By mapping and living this augmented leadership, you help future-proof not just yourself but your entire organization's leadership culture.

In the next final chapter, we will tie everything together into an actionable plan – the **30-Day AI Readiness Action Plan**– which includes steps for leaders and teams to kickstart or accelerate this journey, guided by the principles we've explored throughout the book.

The Human Future

"The best leaders of tomorrow won't be superhuman— they'll be self-aware humans who learn from AI without losing their humanity."
— Futurist Insight

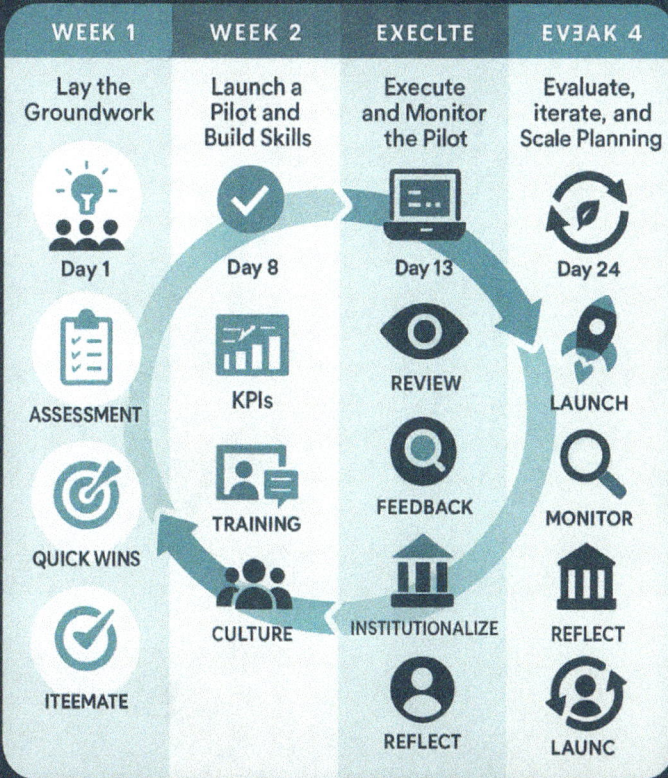

Your 30-Day
AI READINESS ACTION PLAN

WEEK 1	WEEK 2	EXECLTE	EVƎAK 4
Lay the Groundwork	Launch a Pilot and Build Skills	Execute and Monitor the Pilot	Evaluate, iterate, and Scale Planning

Day 1

Day 8

Day 13

Day 24

ASSESSMENT

KPIs

REVIEW

LAUNCH

QUICK WINS

TRAINING

FEEDBACK

MONITOR

ITEEMATE

CULTURE

INSTITUTIONALIZE

REFLECT

REFLECT

LAUNC

Discipline, not destination.

CHAPTER 10 – Your AI Readiness Action

Throughout this book, we've explored the mindset, frameworks, and examples of becoming an AI-ready, human-centered organization. Now it's time to translate insight into action. AI readiness is not a one-time project; it's a continuous discipline of learning and adapting. However, every journey benefits from a strong start. In this concluding chapter, we outline a **30-Day Action Plan** to kickstart your AI readiness initiatives. This is a structured guide for the next month – it can be undertaken by you as an individual leader, or better yet, by your leadership team together. The plan includes assessing your current state, selecting a pilot, engaging stakeholders, establishing metrics, and creating momentum for the long haul. By the end of those 30 days, you won't be "finished" (far from it), but you will have tangible progress and a roadmap to build upon.

Before we dive into the step-by-step plan, remember: **AI readiness is a discipline, not a destination.** The aim is to embed ongoing capabilities – to make your organization adept at continually leveraging new technologies responsibly, rather than checking a box that says "we did AI." Think of this 30-day plan as laying the foundation and scaffolding for a building that will keep rising and evolving.

30-Day AI Readiness Plan: Week-by-Week

Week 1: Lay the Groundwork

Day 1-2: Executive Alignment & Vision Setting

– Hold a kickoff meeting with your key leaders or team to reiterate *why* AI readiness is critical (perhaps share key stats or excerpts from this book, like how 75% of companies have yet to see returns but those who align people, strategy, and AI succeed). Articulate a simple vision or imperative statement, e.g., "We will augment our human intelligence with AI to improve customer experience and operational excellence, while staying true to our values." Gain verbal buy-in. This is also where the *quote* "Tomorrow's leaders won't be replaced by AI—they'll be replaced by leaders who harness its power while amplifying their human wisdom" can be a rallying line – discuss it, ensure the team embraces that mindset.

Day 3-4: Current State Rapid Assessment

– Using tools from Chapter 2, quickly assess where you stand on the AI Readiness Spectrum™ in Strategic, Operational, and Human readiness. You could do a one-hour workshop scoring yourselves on Unaware→Transformative for each domain. Also identify any ongoing AI-related projects in the company (even small ones). The goal is to map out "here's what we have (or don't have) in strategy, data/tech, skills, culture." Document key gaps and strengths. For example, maybe you find operationally you have good data warehouses but human readiness is low (fear, low skills). That highlights where to focus (training, culture) in the plan.

Day 5: Quick Wins Brainstorm

– Gather a cross-functional group (or your core team) to brainstorm potential AI use cases or improvements, focusing on pain points and opportunities surfaced in the assessment. Aim for a short list of 3-5 ideas. Use Chapter 6 guidance to consider impact/feasibility. For instance, you might list: "Automate customer FAQ responses with an AI chatbot," "Use ML to predict maintenance," "AI-enhanced sales lead scoring," etc., plus maybe a foundational task like "Clean up customer data." Even if the ideas aren't fully fleshed out, having candidates sets the stage for prioritization.

End of Week 1 Checkpoint

– Summarize: We have leadership buy-in, a vision statement, a baseline understanding, and a few candidate initiatives. Communicate this succinctly to stakeholders (maybe a brief email like "Team, we've embarked on our AI readiness journey, here's what we've done in week 1 and why it's exciting..." – setting a positive tone).

Week 2: Launch a Pilot and Build Skills

Day 6-7: Prioritize and Pick a Pilot
– Using criteria from Chapter 6 (impact, alignment, feasibility), select one initiative as your pilot project. Possibly it's the chatbot, as those often have clear ROI and moderate effort. Or whatever fits your context. Also identify the project lead and core team. Simultaneously, decide on any enablers to tackle (like if you choose predictive maintenance pilot but data sensors are lacking, maybe you pivot to something with readily available data). The key is to choose something achievable within a few months and meaningful if successful.

Day 8: Define Pilot Success Metrics
– Before diving into build, clearly define what success looks like (Chapter 8 guidance). Decide on 2-3 KPIs for the pilot and targets. E.g., "Chatbot to resolve 50% of FAQs with 90% CSAT" or "Lead scoring to improve conversion by 5% within pilot group." Also define pilot scope (e.g., chatbot for one product line only initially, or lead scoring just for one sales team). Document these.

Day 9-10: Assemble Resources & Training
– Ensure you have the right people and tools lined up. Assign staff or recruit a small cross-functional

team for the pilot (e.g., an IT person, a business process owner, maybe a vendor or consultant if needed). Provide just-in-time training: if using a specific AI platform, have team members do a quick online tutorial or bring an expert for a day. Also brief them on ethical guidelines (e.g., how to handle customer data). At the same time, start upskilling beyond the pilot team: announce some training resources available to all, maybe set up accounts on an e-learning platform or schedule an AI 101 session for employees. This addresses the "Human readiness" gap proactively.

Day 11-12: Culture Kickoff

– Do something to engage the broader organization culturally. Perhaps launch an "AI Readiness Pulse Survey" (Chapter 4) to gauge current attitudes, signaling that employee thoughts matter. Or hold a town hall where you share the vision and pilot plan, invite questions (fear to curiosity move). Possibly start an internal newsletter or Slack channel about "AI in [Company]" to share progress and educate. The idea is to create awareness and openness – you don't want people hearing "there's an AI project" through rumors and feeling threatened; instead they hear it from leadership positively and know how they can be involved or learn.

End of Week 2 Checkpoint
– By now you've got a pilot project officially kicked off with goals and a team, and you've initiated training and communication efforts to involve everyone. Check: is anything blocking progress? If, say, a needed tool is not procured, expedite that via management clout now.

Week 3: Execute and Monitor the Pilot

Day 13-15: Pilot Development Sprint
– The team should begin building/configuring the AI solution. If it's something like a chatbot, maybe by Day 15 they have a basic version working with a few common questions. If lead scoring, they might have gathered historical data and started training a model. The key for leadership is to remove obstacles and keep them focused. Possibly use agile methods (daily stand-ups etc.). Also ensure ethical considerations are checked (e.g., review bot responses for any bias or tone issues now; for lead model, check it's not inadvertently targeting based on sensitive attributes).

Day 16: Mid-Pilot Review
– Even if the pilot isn't done, hold a brief review with stakeholders of interim progress. Are we on track to meet our metric targets? (Maybe not measured yet, but see if anything worrying, like "the bot is struggling with more queries than

expected, might need more training data"). Also gather initial feedback from any users involved in testing so far. Use this to adjust: maybe you realize you need to narrow the chatbot scope because certain complex queries are too hard, so you decide those will still go to humans. That's fine; better to refine early than disappoint later.

Day 17-18: Team Upskilling & Adaptation
– Take time to coach pilot team or involved staff on new skills as needed. If a call center rep is helping test the chatbot, teach them how to "train" it by providing answers – that's new for them, but a growth opportunity to become a "bot trainer." Also encourage team members to share what they're learning – perhaps a short internal blog or email: "3 things we learned building our first AI chatbot." This reinforces a learning culture.

Day 19: Expand Involvement
– If feasible, involve a small group of end-users in a controlled test. For chatbot, maybe have 5-10 friendly customers or employees use it and give feedback. For lead scoring, perhaps quietly use scores for one week and see outcomes (with reps aware it's a test). This starts real-world validation. Monitor closely to capture data on those KPI metrics if possible (even if sample small). And watch for any negative surprises.

End of Week 3 Checkpoint
– Ideally by end of week 3, pilot solution is functional in test mode and some preliminary results/feedback have come in. Summarize: e.g., "Chatbot v1 handles 40% of questions correctly, testers are mostly satisfied except for X topic it fails at. We plan to improve X and then launch wider." Or "Lead model preliminary lift is 3%, a bit short of 5% goal – we found it struggles with region Y data, we are retraining with more features." Decide: is another iteration needed before official pilot measurement? Likely yes – schedule that for early Week 4.

Week 4: Evaluate, Iterate, and Scale Planning

Day 20-22: Pilot Iteration & Finalize
– Refine the AI solution based on feedback and testing. Perhaps add that missing data, tweak model parameters, or expand the chatbot knowledge base. Run it again with testers. By Day 22, aim to have a pilot version you'd consider "MVP" (minimum viable product) ready for prime time in the limited scope. Also, at this point ensure supporting materials are ready – e.g., if the chatbot will go live on website for limited users, have help info prepared; if lead scores will be shown to reps, have a one-pager explaining how to use them.

Day 23: Success Criteria Check

– Measure the KPIs with the pilot data you have. Are you hitting, or at least trending towards, the target? Use whatever short timeframe data – maybe chatbot got 50 queries in test, how many resolved? If metrics aren't near target and cannot be with quick fixes, decide if the target or approach needs adjusting. It might be acceptable to launch pilot officially even if at 80% of goal, as long as it's improving and still beneficial. Reiterate definition of success and make sure stakeholder expectations are aligned to the current reality. Document any changes (e.g., "Goal resolution 50%; currently at 40% but with known fixes coming – proceeding with pilot launch but will keep it to certain FAQs until we reach 50%.")

Day 24: Official Pilot Launch and Communication

– Now roll out the pilot in its intended environment (e.g., make the chatbot live to all website visitors of Product X section, or have the sales team start using the scoring in daily routine). Since it's still a pilot, frame it as such. Communicate to those affected: For customers, perhaps label chatbot as beta and invite feedback. For employees, clear instructions and support channels (maybe a dedicated Slack channel for questions/feedback on the tool). If appropriate, issue a short press release or internal news highlighting this milestone: it builds awareness and excitement that "we have our first AI capability live," giving credit to the team that built it. Also reassure – e.g., "This system is here to assist, and our human staff remain fully available for any needs." That addresses any lingering fear.

Day 25-26: Monitor and Support
– Keep a close eye on pilot performance in the first days of launch. The team should be ready to intervene or adjust parameters if something goes awry (like bot misunderstanding something frequently – maybe temporarily remove that topic from its scope). Provide extra support to users – e.g., the sales manager might sit with reps to observe them using lead scores and ensure they trust and use them well. Collect usage data and feedback.

Day 27: Evaluate & Celebrate Pilot Outcomes
– After a few days of live running, convene the leadership team to evaluate the outcomes against the success criteria. Even if the data window is short, you'll have qualitative and some quantitative sense. Discuss: Did this pilot achieve enough to proceed to a larger scale or to new projects? What did we learn? Perhaps you find an unforeseen benefit (maybe customers loved a feature you didn't expect, or an employee found a creative new use for the tool). Also be honest about what didn't work and why. Capture these lessons.

Importantly, **celebrate** reaching this point – this might be the first AI project delivered for your org, which is a big cultural step regardless of size. Thank the team, acknowledge contributors, share positive results (e.g., "in 3 days, chatbot handled 300 queries – that's 300 faster answers we delivered!" or "sales team closed 2 deals aided by lead scores already, a promising start"). This reinforcement builds momentum.

Day 28: Decision & Scale Gameplan
– Make an informed decision: is the pilot going to scale, be extended, or need overhaul? For instance, you might decide "Yes, let's roll out chatbot to the entire support site over next 2 months with improvements and more training content." Or "We'll keep pilot running another month to hit KPI consistently, then scale." If the pilot was not successful, decide whether to pivot to another approach or idea – but even then, identify positive takeaways (e.g., "We realized our data infrastructure needs fixing – that's our next step before another AI attempt."). Outline a gameplan for scale or next steps, including timeline, responsible persons, and resources needed (budget for more licenses, hiring data engineer, etc.). Also consider if this pilot revealed any new opportunity or need for policy (like data governance or an AI ethics committee if not in place – maybe minor now but plan for it).

Day 29: Institutionalize & Integrate

– Start integrating the pilot knowledge into the organization's processes. For example, add the pilot metrics to the regular management dashboard so they continue to be tracked. Update SOPs (standard operating procedures) or employee guidelines to include how to use the new AI system. If training modules are needed for broader user base, get those scheduled. Essentially, treat the AI solution as part of business as usual going forward – who will maintain it? Ensure that's assigned (maybe the IT or operations owner).

Day 30: Reflect and Reinforce AI Readiness as Ongoing

– Take time to reflect with the leadership team on the journey of the last 30 days. What surprised you? How did people react? Are there skeptics turned supporters (or vice versa)? Use this to reinforce that AI readiness is an ongoing practice. Perhaps document this journey in a brief report or presentation to share company-wide, highlighting lessons and next initiatives. Emphasize the discipline aspect: maybe you commit to a quarterly AI readiness review meeting to maintain momentum, or create an internal "AI task force" that will guide multiple projects. On Day 30, also plan immediate next steps beyond this month: maybe starting another pilot from your idea list, or expanding upskilling programs based on interest sparked.

Now you have not only accomplished a concrete project, but also set in motion structural changes: A more educated workforce, a success story (or at least a valuable experience), the beginnings of a data-driven culture, and a leadership cadence around AI.

Throughout this plan, one final piece is crucial: **maintaining the human-centered focus**. Continuously solicit feedback – "How do employees feel about the changes?" "How are customers responding?" Check that no one is feeling left behind; address concerns swiftly to show that you pair innovation with empathy. For example, if one support rep feels the chatbot threatens their role, have a manager talk with them about how their role can evolve (maybe handling more complex cases or managing the bot's content – turning fear into ownership).

In summary, by taking decisive yet considerate steps over 30 days, you can break the inertia and get your organization on the path of AI readiness. The discipline you build – of aligning strategy, nurturing skills, iterating with pilots, measuring results, and scaling ethically – will serve you well beyond any single technology trend. AI readiness is not a destination because technology will keep evolving; but if you embed this adaptive capability, your organization will ride the waves of change rather than be washed over by them.

As you conclude this 30-day sprint and look to the horizon, remember why we do this: not to chase shiny objects, but to better serve our customers, empower our people, and fulfill our purpose in a changing world. The organizations that lead the AI century will indeed be those that invest equally in human and artificial intelligence, as we set forth from the start of this book. They will be led by people like you – leaders who build trust, clarity, and curiosity, and in doing so, define not only company success but humanity's future with AI.

Letter to Future Leader

Dear Future Leader,

You inherit not just a world transformed by technology, but a responsibility to keep it human.

Artificial Intelligence will shape how we live, learn, and lead. But the future will not be defined by algorithms — it will be defined by you.

In this age of acceleration, your true readiness will not come from your mastery of data, but from your mastery of critical thinking with your sensitive discernment.

Purpose will be your North Star, Know why you build, not just what you build. Every tool should elevate human potential, not replace it.

Ethics will be your anchor. In a world where decisions can be automated, you hold on fiercely to accountability, transparency, and justice.

Empathy will be your signature. Listen before you lead. See people before performance. Remember that every innovation changes not only systems, but also souls.

The mirror you hold to AI is the same mirror you hold to yourself. When you lead with purpose, ethics, and empathy, you become the guardian of what makes intelligence wise.

AI will mirror what it finds in us — it will amplify our humanity. It will mirror our best selves back to us.

So, to you — the architect of tomorrow's organizations, the voice that will guide machines toward meaning, the human who will teach technology to be kind —

Lead with heart. Decide with clarity. And never forget: The future is not something to predict — it is something to protect.

Dr. Farzana Chohan

CONCLUSION

Artificial Intelligence is not an endpoint or a project to finish – it's a new layer of capability that will continuously shape how we live and work. The journey we've undertaken in this book makes one thing clear: **leaders who integrate human and artificial intelligence will drive the most successful and enduring organizations of the future.** They will marry technological prowess with deep humanity – using data to inform vision, automation to elevate human roles, and analytics to accelerate learning, all while upholding ethics and purpose. Conversely, leaders who ignore or mismanage AI – whether through indifference, lack of preparation, or ethical lapses – risk being outpaced and losing the trust of their stakeholders.

By following a human-centered framework for AI readiness, you are future-proofing your organization in the truest sense. You are ensuring that as the machines get smarter, your people do too, and that they focus on uniquely human contributions: creativity, empathy, complex problem-solving, relationship-building. You are cultivating a culture that doesn't fear new tools but asks, "How can we use this to serve better?" – a culture of curiosity and continuous improvement. That cultural readiness is your ultimate competitive advantage, because technologies will come and go, but a resilient learning organization will thrive through them all.

Let's revisit a few core takeaways:

- **AI readiness spans Strategy, Operations, and People.** We saw how true transformation requires aligning AI with strategic goals, embedding it into processes, and fostering an adaptive, skilled workforce. If any one of these pillars is neglected, initiatives will falter. But when all three advance in tandem, you create a reinforcing flywheel of progress.

- **Human intelligence and AI are complementary (HI ↔ AI).** Rather than thinking of AI as replacing human jobs or decisions, view it as augmenting them. Our case studies showed that the best outcomes occurred when AI handled what it's best at – data crunching at scale, pattern recognition – and humans applied judgment, ethics, and empathy. This holds at every level, from frontline employees up to the C-suite.

- **Culture is the fertile soil for AI adoption.** If you cultivate trust, transparency, and participation, your people will embrace AI's potential and even help improve it. If you impose technology without regard to fears or ideas, it will meet silent resistance. We emphasized communication, involvement, and ethical guardrails not just as feel-good measures, but as pragmatic steps for sustainable implementation. As one CIO said, "Culture eats AI strategy for breakfast" – meaning you must get culture on board for strategy to matter. The good news: by engaging your team in this journey, you also strengthen culture itself (through upskilling, empowerment, and shared wins).

- **Measure what matters and learn from it.** We put forward metrics for success – from efficiency gains to ROI. The discipline of measuring forces clarity of purpose and allows you to celebrate tangible progress (like OSF HealthCare's $1.2M savings) as well as quickly identify issues (like bias in a model, or lower-than-expected adoption) so you can adjust. Over time, tracking these metrics will also help you quantify the cumulative impact of AI readiness on your organization's performance – turning skeptics into believers through hard evidence.

- **Ethics and belonging are non-negotiable.** Perhaps one of the most important threads was that we must use AI responsibly and inclusively. We confronted biases, emphasized transparency, and placed human values at the center of AI design. Not only is this the right thing to do, it also builds the trust that fuels adoption and protects your brand. We also saw that a strong sense of belonging – making sure every employee knows they have a future in the AI-enabled organization – leads to higher performance and lower turnover. In short, doing good is good business, especially in the context of AI.

Finally, remember that **AI readiness is a continuous discipline, not a destination**. The technology will keep evolving: new algorithms, new applications, new challenges. There will be wins and there will be pilots that don't pan out. But if you've built a *readiness muscle* – the ability to learn, experiment, and adapt – your organization will weather those with agility. Treat each project as both an implementation and a learning opportunity, as we did through pilots and retrospectives. Encourage your teams to remain curious (as the world changes, so must we). Keep updating your AI Readiness Spectrum self-assessment each year and celebrate moving up the stages, from Experimental to Transformative.

We opened this book with the premise that *leaders who embrace AI will replace those who don't*. Now, armed with knowledge, examples, and an action plan, you are among those poised to embrace it – wisely, ethically, and proactively. As you lead your organization into the AI era, you are not just implementing new tools; you are modeling a new kind of leadership for the digital age: adaptive, data-informed, yet profoundly human at its core. That is perhaps the ultimate form of "future-proofing" – to become the kind of leader and organization that can thrive amid uncertainty and change.

The future is not a fixed destiny that AI will dictate; it is something we will co-create with AI as our partner. By fostering AI readiness, you ensure that *your* organization is one of the co-creators of the future of your industry – not a passive observer, but a shaper of what's to come. As you go forth, remain committed to purpose, to your people, and to continuous learning. Do that, and not only will you future-proof your organization, you will also contribute to a future where AI augments human potential and advances human well-being.

Thank you for taking this journey. Your leadership in this pivotal time will help define what the coming decades look like – for your company and, in small but meaningful ways, for society at large. Stay curious, stay compassionate, and lead on.

ABOUT THE AUTHOR

Dr. Farzana Chohan is a globally recognized thought leader at the intersection of AI Readiness, Leadership, and Belonging Culture. With a doctorate in Management and a professional background as an architect, Dr. Chohan brings a unique multidisciplinary perspective to how organizations design their future. She has served as an advisor to leaders in healthcare systems, educational institutions, fortune 500 companies and non-profits worldwide, helping them align human and artificial intelligence for sustainable excellence.

As the Founder of **Optimize Excellence** and Director of **AiArchitect818**, Dr. Chohan leads a consultancy that specializes in human-centered AI transformation. She is passionate about guiding leaders to not only adopt new technologies, but to also cultivate **inclusive cultures of curiosity and ethics** that amplify the benefits of those technologies. Her previous books and research delve into leadership paradigms, mentoring and creating cultures of belonging – work that earned her honors in the leadership development community.

Dr. Chohan is a sought-after keynote speaker (including a TEDx talk on human-centric innovation) and has been featured in publications for her insights on adaptive leadership and diversity in the tech era. She serves on advisory boards focused on women in healthcare, architecture, science & technology, championing the cause of **"AI for All"**.

In all her endeavors, Dr. Farzana Chohan remains committed to a singular vision: a future where organizations achieve extraordinary outcomes by empowering their people – with the support of AI – to lead with purpose, empathy, and creativity. She firmly believes that while AI may be a powerful tool, it is **human leadership** that will define the trajectory of our shared future.

Connect with Dr. Chohan on LinkedIn or via info@aia818.com to follow her latest work, access free resources, and join a community dedicated to human-centered leadership in the AI age.

CALL TO ACTION

Are you ready to find out how AI-ready your organization truly is?

Here are a few concrete steps you can take right now:

✓ Take the AI Readiness Assessment

Evaluate where your organization stands on the AI Readiness Spectrum across Strategy. Operations, and Human factors.

Start a Pilot in the Next 30 Days

Identify an opportunity from this book with colleaggues. Committing to a pilot.

Engage Your Team in the Conversation

Share a concepts from you colleagues
To gather the thoughts.

Pledge to Lead with Purpose in the AI Age

Champion AI ethics and inclusive imovation

The age of AI-augmented leadership is here.
Will you lead the way?

CALL TO ACTION

Are you ready to find out how AI-ready your organization truly is? Don't let this be just an insightful read – turn it into action. Here are a few concrete steps you can take right now:

- **Take the AI Readiness Assessment:** Evaluate where your organization stands on the AI Readiness Spectrum across Strategy, Operations, and Human factors.

- **Start a Pilot in the Next 30 Days:** Identify one opportunity – however small – where AI could make a positive difference in your team's work, and commit to running a pilot. It could be as simple as automating a spreadsheet report or trying a customer service chatbot on one product line. The key is to *start.* Turn back to Chapter 10's 30-day plan and set Day 1 as tomorrow. There's no better way to build momentum and learning.

- **Engage Your Team in the Conversation:** Share a concept from this book with your colleagues (perhaps in your next team meeting). Ask for their thoughts – "Which of our processes do you find could be improved with AI?" or "What part of your job would you love to offload to an AI assistant so you can focus on more meaningful work?" Encouraging dialogue is the first step to building an AI-curious culture.

- **Pledge to Lead with Purpose in the AI Age:** As a leader, make a personal commitment to champion AI ethics and inclusive innovation. Consider formalizing this by creating guiding principles for AI use in your organization (you can draft them using insights from Chapter 5's Ethical Compass) and sharing them with your team. When employees see leadership setting thoughtful boundaries and aspirations for AI, it builds trust and motivation.

- **Stay Connected and Keep Learning:** The AI field evolves quickly. Subscribe to a reputable AI in business newsletter, join a community of practice (perhaps the **AI Leadership Forum** on AiArchitect818.com, where we host monthly live Q&As and share case studies), and keep learning. Encourage your team to do the same. Make AI readiness a continuous journey.

Your action – or inaction – in this moment will shape your organization's trajectory. **Don't wait** for disruption to force your hand. Take the initiative to future-proof your team and your company now. The tools, frameworks, and stories in this book have given you a roadmap. Now it's in your hands to drive forward.

If you found value in this book, **pass it along** to a colleague or peer in your network who could benefit. Let's create a ripple effect of leaders rising to the challenge of our times, crafting a future where technology and humanity thrive together.

The age of AI-augmented leadership is here. **Will you lead the way?**

(Share your success stories, and / or reach out directly info@aia818.com . We're building a community of AI-ready leaders – and we'd love for you to be a part of it.

ACKNOWLEDGEMENTS

No journey is taken alone, and this book is no exception. I wish to extend my heartfelt thanks to the countless individuals and leaders who shared their experiences, insights, and aspirations about AI readiness with me – your stories and candor were the bedrock of the practical guidance in these pages.

To the forward-thinking executives and teams at client organizations around the world: thank you for trusting me as we navigated uncharted waters together. Your willingness to turn fear into curiosity and to experiment with conviction made our collaborations success stories that others can now learn from.

I am deeply grateful to my research colleagues and mentors in the realms of management, AI ethics, and human-centered design. Your work – often generously cited in this book – provided evidence and depth. Special thanks to those at the Global Centre for AI & Humanity and the Oxford Initiative on AI Readiness, whose studies on organizational preparedness and ethics influenced several chapters.

To my team, friends and peers: you exemplify the very adaptability and learning culture we preach. Thank you for tirelessly refining the AI Readiness Spectrum diagnostic, for running workshops across languages and cultures, and for reminding me daily that belonging and innovation go hand in hand. I'm proud of what we do and how we do it – with purpose and empathy.

I must acknowledge the leaders who allowed me to profile aspects of their transformations (even anonymously) – your bravery in sharing not just triumphs but also missteps provided invaluable lessons for readers. Also, a nod to Lolly Daskal for her powerful quote that set the tone for leadership imperative in the AI era, and to many unnamed pioneers in this field who prove that ethical, human-centric AI leadership is possible and profitable

On a personal note, I thank my family and friends for their unwavering support. To my brother – your belief in blending humanistic values with technological progress is ingrained in every page of this book. To my young nephews – you are my inspiration to continuously learn and lead with heart, so that the future I help shape through my work is one you (and all your peers globally) can flourish in. To a special person in life - for the quiet-help and heartfelt-support, Thank You!

Finally, to every reader of this book: thank you for choosing to lead with purpose in the age of AI. Your commitment to approach AI not with trepidation but with curiosity, responsibility, and humanity gives me immense hope. It has been my honor to share this framework with you. I stand alongside you as we transform fear into curiosity, and curiosity into groundbreaking results, all while holding tight to what makes us human.

Here's to your journey ahead – I acknowledge the courage it takes to truly lead in these times, and I celebrate the impact you will make.

CREDITS: RESEARCH REFERENCE RESOURCES

duperrin.com

Technology adoption kills your digital transformation

saama.com

The AI Readiness Imperative in Clinical Research: Why Change Management Is the Missing Link

medium.com

Ch2: AI Readiness Assessment: Madhusudhan Konda | AI Playbook for Organisations

lollydaskal.com

AI Will Replace You: Leaders Who Refuse to Evolve Will Be Left Behind

altimetrik.com

AI Augments and Human Intelligence: An Evolution

appscrip.com

Benefits Of AI In Healthcare: A Guide For Healthcare Leaders

oxalis.io

The 5 Stages of AI Maturity - Oxalis Solutions

faisalhoque.com

From Code to Compassion: Designing AI With Empathy

mitsloan.mit.edu

Unmasking the bias in facial recognition algorithms

weforum.org

AI value alignment: Aligning AI with human values | World Economic Forum

agility-at-scale.com

AI Readiness Blueprint: Preparing Your Organization for AI Adoption

vationventures.com

AI-Driven Innovation: How to Foster a Culture of AI Adoption in Your Organization | Vation Ventures

aclu-mn.org

Biased Technology: The Automated Discrimination of Facial Recognition | ACLU of Minnesota

hbr.org

The Value of Belonging at Work - Harvard Business Review

ldi.njit.edu

The Big Shift: Building Future Skills Today | The Learning and Development Initiative

recruiter.com

Time to Automate: Managers Are Losing 8 Hours Per Week to Manual Tasks

appscrip.com

Benefits Of AI In Healthcare: A Guide For Healthcare Leaders | Appscrip Blog

forbes.com

A Culture Of Belonging Creates A Team That Thrives - Forbes

slick.plus

Embedding Humanity in the AI Age: Why Empathy is the New Competitive Advantage | Slick +

microsoft.com

Enterprise AI maturity in five steps: Our guide for IT leaders - Inside Track Blog

altimetrik.com

AI Augments and Human Intelligence: An Evolution

www.ingramcontent.com/pod-product-compliance
Lightning Source LLC
Chambersburg PA
CBHW071548200326
41519CB00021BB/6655